Praise for *Your Tax Questions An*

"Ed Slott's easy-to-understand tax strategies mean money in your bank, not the IRS's."
Jan M. Rosen, *The New York Times*

"If thinking about slogging through a huge tax manual gives you a migraine, Slott has the antidote. No matter what your tax concerns, you'll find the answers—and without the usual technical jargon—in this new book."
Susan Berger, financial writer, *Elle* magazine

"Does an excellent job of untangling the rules. Much of the advice will help throughout the year…"
James Kroll, *Cleveland Plain Dealer*

"In person, on the air, and now in print, Ed Slott defies the image of the bookish, out-of-touch CPA. In this new book, Ed takes the rocket science out of tax law…a must read for anyone attempting to understand taxes…"
Raymond G. Russolillo, CPA/PFS, CFP, Director, Personal Financial Services, Price Waterhouse LLP

"Working women need this book to help them through the annual maze of tax preparation and planning."
Alice Bredin, author of the syndicated column "Working at Home"

"Thank you, Ed Slott, for proving that the words 'humor,' 'taxes,' and 'CPA' can exist in the same sentence."
Larry M. Elkin, CPA, author of *Financial Self-Defense for Unmarried Couples*, Doubleday

"A lively book that answers questions people really ask."
Lynn Brenner, *Newsday*

"Makes highly technical tax rules easy to understand…I highly recommend this book for both taxpayers and tax advisors."
Seymour Goldberg, CPA, MBA, JD, author of J.K. Lasser's *How to Pay Less Tax on Your Retirement Savings*, Macmillan

"Direct, upbeat answers will make you eager to manage your tax bill."
Nadine Gordon Lee, CPA, Senior Vice President, U.S. Trust Company

More praise for *Your Tax Questions Answered*...

"Tax books are usually the best cure for insomnia. Ed Slott's new book is the exception. His lively style, question-and-answer format, and logically organized presentation make this an essential handbook for the fiscally challenged."
    Stephen Davies, President, U.S. Computer Group and *INC* magazine's 1995 Entrepreneur of the Year

"I am most impressed... Ed Slott's new book answers questions on some of the most critical issues faced by taxpayers. The section on pension distribution planning alone makes it a worthwhile investment."
    Sidney Kess, CPA, Attorney at Law, and noted tax authority

"Easy-to-read, informative, and user-friendly. Women business owners in particular will profit from Slott's valuable advice."
    Suzanne Israel Tufts, President and CEO, American Woman's Economic Development Corporation

"A lively approach to tax preparation advice...deals with issues where others fear to tread."
    James L. Craig, Jr., CPA, Managing Editor, *The CPA Journal*

"Ed Slott has transformed the esoteric into an easy-to-read compendium of the right answers to the right questions."
    Laurence I. Foster, CPA/PFS, partner, KPMG Peat Marwick LLP, Personal Financial Planning Group

"Injects personality and wit into a subject which most people equate with going to the dentist...makes the dreaded approachable and even embraceable."
    Joseph V. Falanga, CPA, Partner, Goldstein Golub Kessler & Co., P.C.

"An invaluable tool for the savvy woman business owner. He relates to us with respect..."
    Ginger Broderick, CPA, New York, NY

Your Tax Questions Answered

A CPA with over twenty years of experience answers the most commonly asked tax questions

by
Ed Slott, CPA

© 1998 Edward A. Slott, CPA

ISBN 1-882663-16-0

Plymouth Press, Ltd.
42500 Five Mile Road
Plymouth, MI 48170-2544

Copy-editing by Jan Jones
Editorial assistance by Ashley Andersen

All Plymouth Press books are available at a significant discount when purchased in bulk quantities for educational or promotional purposes. Special promotional editions can be formulated to fulfill specific needs. Call our marketing manager at (800) 350-1007 for further information.

All rights reserved. No part of this publication may be reproduced, stored in a retrieval system, or transmitted in any form by any means without the prior written permission of Plymouth Press, Ltd.

Your Tax Questions Answered has been carefully researched to provide accurate and current data to taxpayers. Readers are cautioned, however, that the Publisher is not engaged in providing accounting, legal, or other professional services. If such services are required, then readers are advised to seek the aid of a competent tax professional.

*Dedicated to my wife Linda,
and our dear children, Jennifer, Ilana, and Rachel.*

Contents

Foreword 8
An Iconic Note 9
Summary of '96-'97 Tax Law Changes 10
1 *Your Big Picture Tax Questions* 13
2 *Your Questions About Getting Ready to File* 19
3 *Your Taxing Questions About Your Income* 35
4 *Your Tax Deduction Questions* 47
5 *Your Questions About Home Office Deductions* 71
6 *Your Questions About Your Business and Taxes* 81
7 *Your Questions About Your Marriage and Taxes* 99
8 *Your Questions About Living Together Unmarried* . 107
9 *Your Questions About Divorce and Taxes* 117
10 *Your Questions About Your Home and Your Vacation Home* 125
11 *Your Questions About Your Audit* 137
12 *Your Questions About Your Pensions and IRAs* 145
13 *Your Questions About Your Social Security Benefits and Taxes* 173
14 *Your Estate Planning and Taxes* 179
Appendix A *What's the difference between?...* 197
Appendix B Table: *How the new tax law treats IRA withdrawals....* 204
Acknowledgments 205
Index 209
About the Author 217

Foreword

As a CPA with more than 20 years experience preparing tax returns, I seldom hear a question I haven't heard before, or one for which I don't have a ready answer. Yet, I have to admit, that sometimes even I am amazed by what my clients can come up with.

To guide my clients—and you—I have compiled the answers to the most commonly asked tax questions I face in my busy everyday practice. In this new 1998 edition, I have taken care to cover the new tax laws relating to such topics as newly available tax credits for children and education expenses, Roth IRAs, and changes in estate tax law. But I haven't neglected to cover the issues which have the biggest impact on everyone's financial and emotional well-being, such as:

- *Your home and taxes*
- *Home office deductions*
- *Tax deductions* (I've got some you probably haven't thought of)
- *Marriage: tax implications*
- *Taxes when you're living together, whether you're young, middle-aged, or retired*
- *Divorce: tax implications*
- *Audits*
- *Your pension and IRA accounts*
- *Small business tax issues*
- *Estate planning*

In this book you'll find direct answers to your questions without sleepy tax talk or layered legalese. Even if you're experienced, smart, and in the hands of a seasoned tax professional, you'll find answers to some pretty important tax questions that you haven't had the time to worry about—yet.

The goal of this book is to make a complicated subject easy to understand, maybe even fun. You don't have to be a tax expert to read this book, you only have to be a taxpayer.

An Iconic Note

To make *Your Tax Questions Answered* even easier to use this year, I've added margin icons to help you identify areas of special interest or concern. Here they are:

Hot tip!
A tax tip of special note or importance

Tax trap!
A tax that you should avoid or could easily miss paying

Good tax law
Hey, I do want to give the guys in Congress their due: sometimes they get it right

Bad tax law
Uh, oh! The guys in Congress have been unclear or unfair

New tax law will affect 1997 returns
New tax law will take effect on current 1997 returns

New tax law will affect future returns
Plan now to make the most of coming attractions from Congress

Really stupid tax law
Congress has really outdone themselves with this stinker

Summary of Recent Tax Law Changes
With cross-references to question and answers...

Changes affecting your current 1997 return

Tax Relief on Gains from Home Sales and from Investments
- *Home sales* **Questions #147-#151**
- *Other capital gains* **Question #28**

Pension and IRA Tax Changes
- *Spousal IRAs increased to $2,000* **Question #181**
- *Penalty-free IRA withdrawals for medical expenses* **Question #184**
- *Medical Savings Accounts* **Question #197**
- *Deferral of required distributions for workers more than 70½ years of age* **Question #191**
- *Repeal of pension excise tax* **Question #193**
- *Repeal of $5,000 death benefit* **Question #189**
- *New SIMPLE accounts created* **Question #198**

Other
- *Adoption tax credit* **Question #68**
- *Long term care deduction* **Question #60**
- *Loss of tax benefits due to missing Social Security or Tax Identification Numbers* **Question #10**
- *Home office deduction for storage space* **Question #79**
- *Increase in First-year Expensing* **Question #104**
- *Re-electing S Corporation status* **Question #88**
- *Expatriation rules* **Question #212**
- *Damage recoveries for non-physical injuries* **Question #24**

Changes which will take effect on future returns

Estate Tax Changes
- *The federal estate tax exemption gradually increases from $600,000 in 1997 to one million dollars in 2006* **Question #209**
- *Family business tax break* Beginning in 1998, the first $1.3 million of value of a family farm or business will be exempt from federal estate tax. **Question #215**

- *Installment payment of estate tax* Beginning in 1998, the interest rate paid on estate tax paid in installments drops to 2%, but is no longer deductible (the previous 4% interest was deductible). **Question #215**
- *Living Trust tax relief* Effective for decedents dying after August 5, 1997, gifts made from living trusts within three years of death can no longer be brought back into the estate of the grantor (the person who set up the living trust). **Question #221**

Education Tax Credits
- *HOPE Tax Credit* **Questions #42, #43, and #48**
- *Lifetime Learning Credit* **Questions #42, #43, and #47**

Individual Retirement Accounts (IRAs)
- *The new Roth IRA and Roth IRA conversion of traditional IRAs* **Questions #169-174**
- *Penalty-free withdrawals for first time home-buyers and for education* **Questions #171-#178**
- *Active participant rule change* Beginning in 1998, you may make a deductible IRA contribution if your spouse is an active participant in a company pension while you are not. **Question #182**
- *Increase in phaseout range* Beginning in 1998, the new law gradually increases the income limit for tax-deductible contributions to an IRA to $80,000 in the year 2007 (if married joint) and $50,000 in the year 2005 (single or head of household). **Question #182**
- *Repeal of five-year averaging* **Question #188**
- *Education IRAs* Beginning in 1998, you can contribute up to $500 to a nondeductible IRA for each child under 18 years old. **Questions #42 and #46**

Other
- *Child tax credits* Beginning in 1998, a $400 tax credit is available to parents for each child under 17 years old. The credit increases to $500 in 1999. **Question #66**
- *Deduction for student loan interest* Beginning in 1998, some of the interest paid by students and parents of students on student loans will be deductible, increasing gradually up to $2,500 in 2001. **Question #42**

- *Home office* Beginning in 1999 the tax law has been amended to make it easier to qualify for home office deductions. **Introduction to Section 5, page 71**
- *Deduction for health insurance for self-employed individuals* The deduction for 1997 stays at 40%, but then goes up over 10 years to 100% in 2007. **Question #94**
- *Standard mileage deduction rate for charitable purposes* In 1997, it's 12 cents per mile. In 1998, it will go up to 14 cents per mile. **Question #56**
- *The exclusion for employer-provided educational assistance* The exclusion for employer-provided educational assistance will increase. **Question #41**
- *New estimated tax rules* **Questions #12, #14, and #30**
- *Electronic tax deposit relief* **Question #101**

Section 1
Your Big Picture Tax Questions

There is one difference between a tax collector and a taxidermist—the taxidermist leaves the hide.

Mortimer Caplan, former Commissioner, Internal Revenue Service

Getting ready for your taxes? Are you sure you don't want to take care of that root canal first? Actually, taxes are not that bad if you get an early jump on them. But the closer it gets to Tax Super Bowl day, April 15, the more the pressure and tension increase dramatically on you—and your accountant.

There is some tax document collection and organization that you should do ahead of time, even if you hire a professional tax preparer. Using questions my clients have posed to me over the years, I'll take you through all of that. I'll identify items that often delay returns and, in many cases, your refund.

I try to educate my clients. But no matter how hard I try, there are always those who, when we sit down to organize their tax return, still need a laundry list of items. This section covers that list so you can avoid that time-consuming—and costly—second trip to your accountant.

You're off… Good luck!…see you at the finish line!

1. How long must I keep my tax records?

Some people devote a whole room to storage of tax documents because of the possibility that someday they may be asked to prove something or other that will make it all worthwhile. You might not have to. There is no official list of what you must keep, but here are the recommendations I make to my clients:

Records you should keep
1. *Tax returns* **Permanently**

I recommend to my clients that they keep their tax returns forever. Sometimes they provide the only evidence that you filed. I'm not talking about all the attachments and receipts, just the actual tax forms themselves. Tax returns contain so much information that they should never be discarded.

You can actually recreate your entire life from these things, but don't try—unless you have no life.

Examples of important information tax returns may supply:

- *Information on depreciation of some properties, which may go back as far as 40 years, and will be needed when the properties are sold or disposed of*
- *Tracking of nondeductible IRA contributions*
- *Tracking of reinvested dividends from stocks or funds you acquired years ago and are now selling*
- *Proving earnings to obtain Social Security* In 1990, my father applied to receive Social Security. When they gave him his earnings history to show how they had come up with his monthly benefit, they left out 1979, stating that he had no earnings that year. He presented them with a copy of his 1979 tax return, and they promptly corrected their error and credited his account.

Although the statute of limitations for most federal tax returns is three years, it can be extended to six years for "substantial" (more than 25%) underreporting of income. And there is no statue of limitations for fraud.

2. *Bank statements* **7 years**

This also includes canceled checks, which may be needed to prove tax payments. Some canceled checks should be kept even longer than seven years to verify major purchases, home improvements, or stock or business investments that you still hold. You may need them to prove your cost for figuring gain or loss when you sell.

3. *Loan records* **7 years**

This includes mortgages and any other loans. Keep payment records and loan documents.

4. *Property records* **Permanently**

This includes the deed to your home, records of home improvements, depreciation schedules (if any), blueprints, surveys, plans, appraisals, and copies of Form 2119 (for home sales or rollovers of gain on home sales) on every home you have owned.

5. *Investment information* **3 years after sale**

You need to keep records of purchases and sales of stocks, mutual funds, bonds, and any other investments you hold. If your broker or mutual fund provides you with a complete year-end statement, one that details the entire year's investment activity, not just totals, you only have to keep the year-end statement. You can dump all those monthly and quarterly statements that have already put a claim on space in your home.

6. *Earnings records* **7 years**

This includes W-2 forms and pay stubs. Here, too, as with the investment year-end statements mentioned above, if you receive one detailed year-end statement from your employer, that is all you need to keep. You can trash all those weekly or monthly pay stubs.

② I'm tired of paying tax! What is everything I can do to avoid every kind of tax?

Everyone asks some version of this question. People often seem compelled to do everything and anything to minimize their taxes, even when it may not make sense. You cannot let taxes control your life and your otherwise well thought-out decisions. Some folks go a little too far to reduce their tax bill. Here are a few examples:

"Tax-free"
People sometimes go overboard for tax-free income, their reasoning being that they will lower their taxes. "Triple tax-free" bonds provide income that is exempt for federal, state, and city taxes. But if you live outside the city, you don't pay city taxes, what's the value of being exempt from a tax you don't pay anyway?

Also, if you're buying tax-exempt bonds to avoid the taxation of up to 85% of Social Security benefits (see *Question #203*), it won't work. The tax-exempt income is added back to the amount used to determine how much of your benefits will be taxed.

Big home mortgage
One of the best tax breaks around is the deduction for interest paid on a home mortgage. Unfortunately, to some people, that means taking on

more mortgage debt than they can afford, simply because it's tax-deductible. Saving taxes should not be the only reason for buying a home.

Home equity loans
The interest on the first $100,000 of home equity debt is also tax-deductible. Does this mean everyone should have home equity debt? *No!* A common mistake is using home equity debt to pay off credit card debt. Theoretically this may appear to be a good move since you're replacing the nondeductible personal interest associated with the credit card debt with deductible home equity interest. Practically speaking, though, this may be the beginning of the end, because many people run those credit cards right back up and then have home equity loans as well as credit card debts to pay. This strategy only works for the extremely well-disciplined.

Variable annuities
The income tax deferral on variable annuities is alluring to investors. These investments, however, are not for the short term. Many companies charge a surrender fee if you withdraw your money too soon (within the first 7 to 10 years). There are also IRS penalties for taking the money out before age 59½, in addition to the regular income tax you will owe.

Tax shelters: limited partnerships
Otherwise astute investors have had their minds turned to mush by the thought of beating the tax man. For example, limited partnerships are offering tax credits by investing in low-income housing. Think about it. Would you invest your money in a neighborhood that you would be afraid to walk through just to take advantage of the low-income housing tax credit? Yet these partnerships are selling like hotcakes to investors who have had their good judgment clouded by taxes.

Tax-free IRA investing
Let's keep this one short. Traditional IRA money is already tax-deferred, and Roth IRA distributions are meant to be tax-free. Don't invest IRA money in municipal bonds because you are accepting a lower interest rate in exchange for not having to pay income tax. This is no place for municipal bonds.

Holding on for long-term capital gains
Capital gains breaks have finally arrived. This will make it more attractive to sell investments which have increased in value. (See *Question #28*

for details on the new capital gains rates.) But don't sell just for the tax break. You invested to make money, not to save taxes.

Remember: although taxes play an important role in many financial decisions, don't let them replace your good judgment.

3 **I have heard that the IRS can help me prepare my taxes. This sounds great! How do I get them to help?**

Oh, sure, the IRS is ready to help, but don't expect any miracles. Studies have shown that advice from the IRS, amazingly enough, is often wrong. Who says they don't have a sense of humor? But seriously, there is some good stuff available, especially from the IRS site on the World Wide Web. Here's how to reach out and touch the IRS:

- *IRS internet site: http://www.irs.ustreas.gov* You can download tax forms to your computer and access IRS publications.

- *IRS by phone: (800) 829-3676* All tax forms and tax publications on a variety of topics may be ordered free. A good way to start is with Publication 910, "Guide to Free Tax Services."

- *CD-ROM with over 600 tax forms and instructions, and IRS tax publications* To obtain, call (202) 512-1800. Price: $25.

- *IRS toll-free for the hearing impaired: (800) 829-4059* Use of this resource requires a teletypewriter/communications device for the hearing impaired. Monday to Friday only.

- *IRS Tele-Tax system with recorded tax information on over 100 different tax topics* A list of topics covered and local numbers for access are available in Publication 910, mentioned above.

Hot tip!

Section 2
Your Questions About Getting Ready to File

Luck is a matter of preparation meeting opportunity.
   Oprah Winfrey

Get out the *Maalox* and the *Tagamet*. Everyone knows that preparing for tax time is a year-round task, but somehow many of my clients end up squeezing most of their work into the last few months. (Weeks? Days? Hours? *Minutes?*) But before you or your tax preparer touch pencil or pen to tax form there's a myriad of tasks that have to be completed. That's the focus of this section. I'll explain here to recoup deductions from previous years that you forgot to claim, how to get the most out of your tax preparer when you meet, and some nitty-gritty issues like what to do when you don't have the money to pay the IRS.

If you file an amended return with a deduction which gives you a refund from a return originally filed five years ago, will the IRS pay you interest? (You might be surprised by the answer.) And when can you stop filing returns?

I'll also explain the infamous "Nanny Tax" which applies to employees who work in your household. Oh, I could go on and on…

4. I just realized that I missed a big tax deduction on last year's return. How long do I have to claim my refund?

Three years from the date your original return was filed, including extensions, or two years from the date you actually paid the tax, whichever is later.

The amended return is filed on Form 1040X, and is really pretty simple, but you must provide an explanation of why you're amending your return. Don't forget about filing an amended state return as well—you may also be owed money there. Although the IRS tells your state when you owe money (they call it reciprocity), they do not follow the same procedure when they owe you money. What a surprise!

Hot tip!

Little known exceptions
Of course, every rule has an exception, especially tax rules. When amending your return to claim a loss for worthless securities (stocks, stock **rights,**

bonds, etc.) and non-business bad debts (when you get stiffed on a personal loan you made), you have up to seven years from the date your original return for that year had to be filed, or two years from the date you paid the tax, whichever is later, to claim your refund on an amended return. Where else can you find really cool tax facts like these? Now, aren't you glad you bought this book?

5 Will filing an amended return cause an audit?

Possibly, since most amended returns are filed for refunds, rather than for reporting additional income. The amended return will probably be reviewed manually by an IRS agent, who will decide if it should be examined.

An amended return does not mean an automatic audit. It all depends on the type of change you're making and how much of a refund you're claiming. The higher the refund, the greater the chances of the IRS questioning the added deductions. If the change is a minor amount or a relatively easy item to check, you should not have a problem.

However, if the changes involve large losses or missed deductions, there is an increased chance of an audit. The kinds of added deductions that will more likely trigger an audit of your amended return are: large casualty losses; meals, travel and entertainment deductions; large contributions (especially of highly-appraised property); business expenses on a Schedule C; tax shelter losses or related deductions; and any deductions which involve relatives. If you need to amend any of these items, send as much documentation and explanation as you can with the amended return. This may help avoid an audit.

The safer items are things like: math mistakes that are easy to check, tax credits that were missed, or changing from separately filed returns to joint returns.

6 Do I receive interest on a refund claimed on an amended return if it's my mistake?

Good tax law

Yes. The fact is, the IRS had the use of your money and they'll pay you for that use.

Interest is paid from the due date of your original return or the date you filed your original return, whichever is later, to the date you filed your amended return. The IRS must pay you within 45 days from the date you file your claim or they'll owe interest right up to the date your refund is paid to you.

❼ Rather than amending my 1996 return for a deduction I missed, can I simply claim it on this year's return?

Nope. No way.

❽ I can't pay the tax I owe. Could you prepare an extension for me to file?

Yes, but this is no magic solution to not being able to pay your income tax. When you file for an extension, you must give the IRS an accurate estimate of how much tax you think you owe for the extension to be valid. And the IRS will expect you to pay interest on any tax owed. Think about it. If you could get an interest-free loan from the IRS by delaying payment of your tax, everyone would want one and no one would ever pay on time.

You're entitled to two regular extensions of time to file. The first one is automatic (you don't need to come up with any excuse here). This is a four month extension to August 15. The second extension is not automatic. For this one you need approval, and to get it you need to come up with something better than, "Someone broke into our home and stole our tax information." Quite often the reason may simply be that you are "waiting for additional tax information needed to properly prepare your return." If granted, and it usually is, the second extension gives you two more months—up to October 15. After that, you'd better have a great story. If it works, I would love to hear it.

If you cannot pay the tax, you may file Form 9465 to request an installment payment plan with the IRS. They will contact you within 30 days and let you know if they accept it. If things are really bad and you can show that paying the tax would cause a severe hardship (when doesn't it?), you may file Form 1127 and the IRS may grant you up to a six-month extension to pay. Even if the IRS works out a payment plan or grants you an extension of time to pay, you'll still be obligated to pay them interest on the late payments.

9. What should I do to get the most out of my tax preparer?

Organize! Of course, you could just throw everything in a box and dump it on your accountant's desk. After all, that's what you pay her or him for. It's certainly a good way to keep your accountant busy, and we can all use the business. But the bottom line is that if your information is neat and organized, your return will be completed more quickly—and less expensively. Seriously, your tax preparer's precious time is best spent answering your tax questions and giving you advice that can save you money, not in organizing your paperwork.

10. What kinds of information do I need to provide to my tax preparer to make sure he or she can complete my return as soon as possible?

Deductions

The best way to put your deduction information together is by category. For example, if you have business or work-related deductions, sort them by the type of deduction, examples being: auto expenses, office supplies, repairs, and insurance. Charitable contributions should be another significant category. Home mortgage interest, state income tax withholdings, and state income tax obligations from the previous year paid this year, and local and property taxes are other numbers you'll need. You get the idea. I'll have a lot more to say about deductions in Section 3, which I devoted to the subject. Being organized will also keep you well-prepared in case, horror of horrors, you're audited.

Contribution statements

Contributions of $250 or more at one time to any organization require written substantiation from the charity. Although you do not have to attach this statement to your tax return, you must have it by the date you file your return. The same type of statement is required for contributions in excess of $75 if you received something of value in return, for example, a dinner, or tickets to a show. Although most groups are good about providing this information, be sure you have what you need by the time you file (see *Question #58*).

1099 forms

The 1099 form is one of the ways the government checks up on you. Remember that every time you receive a 1099, the IRS already has a copy, and just like Santa, will be checking it twice. If you don't report your 1099 income, you'll be contacted for an audit or asked to explain why it was omitted from your return. The 1099 form covers a variety of transactions, including interest, dividend, and rental income; fee and business income; securities sales; barter transactions; the proceeds from the sale of your home; and retirement plan distributions. The IRS matches the 1099 forms with your Social Security number. Make sure you keep the 1099s in a safe place and have them all available so that your tax preparer can review and record them.

Stock transactions and buy slips for stocks

For stock sales, make sure you have a year-end 1099-B form for each brokerage account you have. Each stock sale during the year will be reported to the IRS by the broker. You need to supply your tax preparer with the original cost (including reinvested dividends) and the date you bought all the shares sold during the year.

If you sold any stocks during the year, you must report the sale on your tax return. To find the right basis (your cost) to use in figuring your capital gain or loss, you will need your original buy slips or some other record which proves how much you paid for the stock. Don't forget to add back to your basis any reinvested dividends that you paid tax on in previous years (see *Question #35*). Start early, because tracking these may take some time.

If you inherited your stock, remember to use the estate tax value (the step-up in basis) that can relieve a large portion of the gain (see *Question #33* for details).

Pension and IRA rollovers

A rollover occurs when pension or IRA funds are transferred from one tax-deferred account to another. Even though, as far as you're concerned, nothing has really happened, the transaction is reported to the IRS as a distribution by the plan custodian (bank, broker, or mutual fund) from which the money has been transferred. The IRS doesn't know that you actually completed the rollover to a new IRA or pension account unless you tell them, and if you don't tell them, they'll see it as an unexplained distribution. Failure to provide this information to the IRS can trigger an audit, especially if the rollover is large.

Early in the year you will be receiving your W-2s, 1099 forms, and other important tax information. If you're missing anything, don't wait until April 12. The best way to prepare is to start tracking down those hard-to-find items now, so your return won't be delayed. Here are some things you may need that could take more time to obtain than you'd think:

No Social Security number for dependents?...No exemption!

The law has changed once again on this. Beginning in 1997, you will need Social Security numbers for all newborns (even children born on the last day of the year), as well as all others you claim as dependents, regardless of age. (The same goes for dependent care credits.) So for 1997, even if you have a child that was born on December 31, 1997, you still must provide that child's—and other dependent's—taxpayer identification number (TIN), usually the Social Security number, on your 1997 return. So it's a good idea to obtain a Social Security number for your children at birth or as soon as possible thereafter. If you need to apply for a number, file form SS-5 at your nearest Social Security office.

Tax trap!

It gets worse. If you fail to provide the TINs, you not only lose the personal exemptions and credits, but you also lose any of the other tax benefits that are based on the existence of the personal exemptions. For example, if you are eligible to use the tax-favorable filing status of either "Head of Household" or "Qualifying Widow(er)" you will no longer be able to, since they are based on you being able to claim your child or other individuals as dependents.

If you think this is no big deal, think again! The government expects to receive a $2.2 billion windfall from this provision alone.

Child care providers

In order for working parents to benefit from the child and dependent care credit, they must list the care provider's name, address, and tax identification or Social Security number. Sometimes this information is hard to find, especially if it involves a day camp that may be closed for the winter or someone who no longer works for you or who moved out of town. The IRS will not grant the credit without documentation. You will also have to show how much was paid to each care provider.

Medical expenses
If you have had large medical expenses, you may wish to attach a doctor's statement to your return, showing that the medical equipment or treatment was prescribed by him or her.

Work expenses
Start early to hunt down work-related expenses that may take a little longer to collect. If you were unemployed, you may find you need these deductions (especially job-hunting expenses) to offset any unemployment insurance you have received, since this is taxable income.

Recent move or name change
Notify your tax preparer if you move. After all, you want your correct address on your return. Why should the cutthroats who bought your old home end up with your refund check? Second, your preparer should provide you with Form 8822—"Change of Address"—to file with the IRS.

If you changed your name because of marriage or divorce, you should also file Form 8822 (see *Question #133* for details).

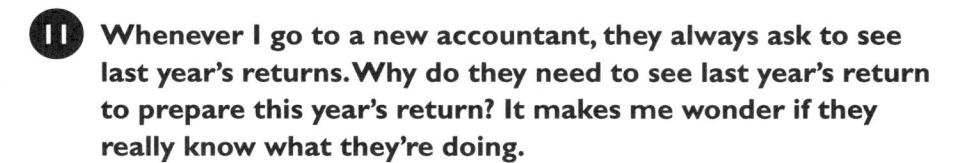

11 **Whenever I go to a new accountant, they always ask to see last year's returns. Why do they need to see last year's return to prepare this year's return? It makes me wonder if they really know what they're doing.**

Whenever I start with a new tax client, I always ask for last year's tax return, not because I want to copy what was done last year or to look for good tax tips, but for a host of other reasons, all of which may benefit you. Here are some of them:

Deductions
Sharp tax preparers always check the prior year's returns to make sure you took all the deductions you were entitled to. After all, we like to be heroes, too, and if we can find a nice juicy deduction you missed, that certainly builds your confidence in our abilities. Many times people miss federal or state deductions. On the federal side, probably the biggest tax deduction overlooked is the deduction for state income taxes paid. Not the ones paid through withholdings on your W-2s or through estimates,

but when you owed money on your state return for the prior year. Did you remember to deduct that state tax payment (but not interest or penalties) on the following year's return?

Example:

Let's say that when you filed for 1996, you found that you owed $842 on your state return. You paid the $842 in owed 1996 taxes in early 1997 when you filed your return. You're then entitled to an itemized deduction for that $842 on your 1997 tax return.

Estimated taxes

Tax preparers will want to see last year's return if you might have a problem with inadequate payment of estimated tax. If you're paying your own taxes through estimates, you're required to have at least 90% of the tax owed in the current year, paid to the IRS by year-end or be subject to a penalty. If you have a large increase in income this year, and end the year owing a substantial amount of tax, you may be exempt from this penalty if you have paid in at least 100% of last year's tax liability (or 110% if your Adjusted Gross Income was over $150,000). You need to look at last year's tax return to see what last year's tax liability was. (See *Questions #12 and #13* for more on the estimated tax penalties and how to beat them.)

Carryovers

There are a number of carryover items that a good tax professional will want to find from last year's or a prior year's return. For example, excess capital losses in prior years from the sale of assets (for example, stocks) can be carried over and be used as a loss on this year's return. Without last year's return, the preparer may not know that they exist—and believe me, and the IRS is not going to remind you!

Net operating losses

These are losses incurred in a business. They often are substantial, especially when start-up businesses incur huge losses in their early years. They can be carried over to subsequent returns.

Passive activity losses

I hate these, and so does every other CPA. I think, deep down, even IRS agents hate this tax area. Luckily, we have computers with super-duper tax programs that somehow compute this stuff—and we sure hope that we're using the same program the IRS does (just joking, we all use the same program). Anyway, the general rule in the passive activity loss area is that if it is laser-printed, then it must be correct.

This is an area that includes a whole myriad and maze of complicated tax rules. In 1986, the government classified real estate and certain other investments as "passive" and said that losses from these activities can generally be taken only against passive income, as distinguished from earned or investment income. Consequently, people who have passive losses from depreciation, for example, must often carry them over until they have passive income. Often, when they sell the passive investment, they have a gain and are able to take the loss against it. You must keep track of these items, so hold onto your old returns.

Depreciation deductions
Since most business property is depreciated over several years, you need to have last year's return—and more—to track these depreciation deductions for the current year.

IRS Section 179, depreciation deductions (see *Question #104*), is another reason to review old returns. For 1997, you can write off up to $18,000 of the cost of business machinery and/or equipment. If you can't use the deduction in the year you bought it, you can carry over the unused deduction to future years. I would have to see the prior year's returns to know that the carryover existed.

Installment sales
Let's say you sold a piece of property on the installment method, meaning that, rather than get all the money at the time of the sale, you get paid in installments over a term of years. You can elect to report the profit, on a percentage basis, on each payment you received for a particular year. I would need to know the history of these payments, including the gross profit percentage, and the only place to find them is on prior years' returns.

Mistakes
The best reason of all for a tax preparer to look at last year's return is to look for mistakes. Maybe there's money coming to you. Wouldn't you want to find out?

12 **My income is up this year. Do I need to increase my estimated tax payments so that I don't end up short and owe a substantial amount when I file my return?**

If the increase in income is from wages, pensions, or other items from which appropriate tax has been withheld, you should be fine. But it is up to you to make up the short fall with estimated tax payments if the income is from sources like the following:

- *Capital gains*
- *Unemployment insurance from which tax is not generally withheld*
- *The 85% of Social Security benefits which count as income for those above certain income levels (see **Question #203**)*
- *For those receiving Social Security benefits, income from municipal bonds which is otherwise tax-free counts toward the level at which the benefits become 85% taxable (see **Question #203**)*

Do you have enough tax paid in?

You're required to have at least 90% of your tax prepaid. You can qualify for an exemption from the underestimation penalty by paying in at least 100% of last year's tax (or 110% if your Adjusted Gross Income exceeds $150,000, or $75,000 if married, filing separately).

Beginning with 1998 tax returns, the new tax law raises from $500 to $1,000 the amount you are allowed to owe before getting hit with an underpayment penalty. But remember that for 1997 returns you must still owe less than $500 in order to avoid the penalty.

Tax trap!

New tax law will affect future returns

13 **My income is up this year from a capital gain on the sale of a piece of property. However, I have never paid estimated taxes since I am an employee and all my taxes have been paid through withholding from my regular wages. The gain is an aberration for me and I don't expect any thing like this in the future. Do I have to start paying estimated taxes now ?**

Don't be so pessimistic. How do you know this is an aberration? Don't you believe in the lottery?

There is an easy solution: using your situation as an employee, you can ask your employer to increase the tax withholding on your wages through

Hot tip!

the end of the year to pay in the extra tax due. If this suffices to pay the extra tax owed, you're in luck—any extra year-end withholding tax payments are considered as paid evenly throughout the year, which is how income tax is supposed to be paid if you want to avoid an underpayment penalty. For example, if your gain was early in the tax year, let's say February, and you waited until your last paycheck in December to take the extra wage withholding, then the withholding tax taken from December would be treated as being paid in evenly throughout the tax year.

If you cannot come up with enough tax through wage withholding, either because the tax is too high or your wages are too low, you must pay an estimated tax that would bring your total taxes paid to at least last year's tax or to an amount equal to 90% of the tax that you will owe. Consider the timing of income like capital gains and pay the estimated tax in the quarter that the large income is realized.

14 I really do want to be Attorney General. What must I do about this darned "Nanny Tax" that applies to everyone I employ in my home?

Suddenly, everybody wants to play by the rules, even political hopefuls. You will be happy to know that Congress has "simplified" the tax rules for employing people in your home.

The new "Nanny Tax" rules for household employees
If you employ people to work in your home, you may be one of the first on your block to be filing the new "Nanny Tax" form. It is now part of your regular tax return (Form 1040), filed on new Schedule H, "House hold Employment Taxes." The form made its debut on 1995 returns.

What is the "Nanny Tax" for household employees?
This is the term commonly used to describe the employment taxes withheld and paid by individuals who hire others to work in their home. It came into prominence when several presidential appointees were denied confirmation by Congress because they failed to pay taxes owed on employees working in their homes.

These taxes are applicable not only to nannies, but to all employees working in and around your home and under your direct control with tools and materials that are supplied by you. In general, this means housekeepers, health-care providers, baby sitters, drivers, caretakers, cooks, private nurses, and cleaning people. However, they do not apply to workers supplied by an agency, who work for the agency and provide services to you as well as to others. The "Nanny Tax" provisions also do not apply to self-employed workers such as gardeners or plumbers, who may work occasionally in your home but also have other customers.

Which taxes?
The taxes owed on wages paid to household employees are: FICA (Social Security), Medicare, withheld federal and state income taxes, Federal Unemployment Tax (FUTA), and, in most states, State Unemployment Tax. Only the first $7,000 of wages are taxable for Federal Unemployment Taxes.

Tax forms to file
This part has been somewhat simplified by the introduction of Schedule H, which replaces much of the quarterly filing requirements, including Form 942. (Reporting on the state level is still on a quarterly basis.) Schedule H is used to report federal employment taxes, which in most cases are filed as part of your regular personal tax return. You must also file W-2 forms for your household employees and Form W-3 to transmit the W-2 forms to the Social Security Administration. Check the "Hshld" box on the W-2 form to indicate that someone is a household employee. When you hire household employees, you must apply for an employer identification number (EIN) and have your employees fill out W-4 forms.

Illegal aliens?
Every household employer must complete Form I-9 for all employees. Form I-9 verifies employment eligibility in the U.S. for the Immigration and Naturalization Service (INS). This form must also be available for inspection by the INS, if requested by their agents. To obtain I-9 forms call 1-(800) 755-0777 and request the INS Handbook for Employers.

Exceptions to the rules
The household employment tax rules do not apply to workers under age 18, unless providing household services is their principal occupation. This rule basically knocks out the tax problem for baby-sitters. Household workers who earn less than $1,000 per year are also exempt. Generally, payments to your spouse, children under age 21, or parents are also ex-

empt from the Nanny Tax rules, including the FUTA tax. As employer, however, you're responsible for FUTA if total household wages exceed $1,000 in any calendar quarter, even if paid to someone who is exempt. Also, check to see if your state requires unemployment taxes on household employees, and whether there is a quarterly filing requirement.

Extension tax trap
The household employment taxes are due by April 15. There are no extensions for the payment of this tax, even though your regular return may be on extension.

Still too complicated
A big problem is that when Congress attempted to lessen the paperwork involved (for which you still need an accountant), they never told the states about it. On the federal level, the rules have been somewhat simplified, but on the state level the quarterly filing requirements are still burdensome. Paying estimated taxes is really the only way to avoid owing a big tax on April 15 if you have full time help or your payroll is substantial. Remember: beginning in 1998 you must include any household employment taxes in your estimated tax payments.

It does not take much to build up a big tax debt. For example, if you have only one person whom you pay, say $200 per week, you will owe combined federal taxes alone of $2,147.20 (see the example which follows) on the $10,400 of annual wages paid. You will add more for state unemployment and income taxes.

Example:
Annual gross wages paid: $10,400
Employer's Social Security tax at 6.2% $644.80
Employee's Social Security tax withheld at 6.2% 644.80
Employer's Medicare tax at 1.45% 150.80
Employee's Medicare tax withheld at 1.45% 150.80
   Federal Unemployment Tax at 0.8% (on the first
   $7,000 of wages) 56.00
Federal tax withheld (estimated and optional) 500.00
Total federal taxes $2,147.20

15 When can I stop filing tax returns? I am retired and do not earn enough to file.

Some taxpayers feel like it would be un-American not to file their tax return. However, if you don't need to, the IRS would rather you didn't, and is sending out letters to some folks suggesting that they may not have to file.

From the IRS

"Dear taxpayer," the letter begins, "You may not have to file a federal tax return this year…" The letter goes on to say, "If you don't have to file a tax return, you'll save time, and if you usually pay someone else to prepare your return, you'll also save money." Is this too good to be true? The fact is, the IRS wants to cut down on needless paperwork both on your part and theirs. They would prefer that you do not file a tax return if you don't have to.

To file or not to file...

Hot tip!

To figure out if you need to file a tax return, there are three exemption amounts you need to know. These are the standard deduction, the extra standard deduction for those 65 and over, and personal exemptions. Based on your filing status (married filing jointly, single etc.), you add the exemption amounts to see how much you would have to earn before you have to file a tax return for 1997.

For example, if you file married-joint, and you and your spouse are both 65 or older, your 1997 income would have to exceed $13,800 for you to have to file a federal tax return. The $13,800 amount includes the 1997 standard deduction of $6,900, the extra standard deduction for those 65 and older of $800 each (for a total of $1600), and the two personal exemptions of $2,650 each. If a husband and wife are both under 65, the amount would be $12,200, because they would not receive the extra standard deductions. For each child or other dependent you claim, however, the amount would increase by $2,650.

Single individuals who are 65 or over must have income in excess of $7,800 before being required to file a federal tax return. This $7,800 amount breaks down to the standard deduction of $4,150 for single filers, the extra standard deduction for singles 65 and older of $1,000, and the personal exemption of $2,650. For those less than 65 years of age, the threshold for filing decreases to $6,800 since they are not eligible for the extra standard deduction.

Although you may not have to file a federal return, you still may have to file a state tax return because some states have lower income thresholds for exemption from filing than the IRS.

When you still have to file
Even though your income may be below the exemption amounts, you may still be required to file if any of the following apply:

- *You sold your home*

- *You had a job and want to get a refund of withheld taxes*

- *You had taxes withheld from an IRA or pension distribution and want to receive a refund of the taxes withheld*

- *You had self-employment income and your net earnings after deductible expenses were $400 or more*

- *You had stock or bond sales*

- *You wish to apply for the earned income credit*

- *You had IRA distributions that are subject to an early withdrawal penalty (you're under 59½ years old)*

16 **Following up on Question #15, what should I do if, when I stop filing, I receive a notice from the IRS asking where my return is? I really don't want to end up in a letter-writing campaign that may outlive me.**

This is exactly what people worry about…and it does happen. If you receive one of those IRS letters that let you know that you may not have to file and you take the IRS's advice to stop filing, there is a chance that you will receive a letter from a different IRS department asking for your "missing" return. If that happens, IRS spokesperson Robert Kobel says "Don't get upset, simply write back that you're not required to file because your income is under the exemption amounts, and that should be the end of it. The IRS really does not want you to file unnecessarily."

Section 3
Your Taxing Questions About Your Income

I have long been of the opinion that if work were such a splendid thing the rich would have kept more of it for themselves.
  Bruce Grocott

Income is a funny thing. You like to have lots of it, but you hate to share it with the government. Unfortunately, most income is taxable and must be reported on your return. But every cloud has a silver lining, so it's nice to know that there are some types of income that aren't taxable.

If you are mistakenly planning to pay a tax on income that you didn't have to report, this section may save you. And don't worry—the IRS won't bother you about having paid tax on income that you don't need to pay tax on. (But they are pretty good at letting you know when it goes the other way.) At least once a year I come across situations where people have paid huge taxes on income that should never have been reported.

On the other hand, if you're now unaware that other types of income are taxable, this section will save you from that thoughtful reminder (with interest and penalties) that the IRS will be sending you.

So reading this section will save you from tax traps, and maybe help you from sharing some of your hard-earned income with Uncle Sam.

17 Why do I have to report my state income tax refund as income? Isn't that double taxation?

No. When you deducted the total of state income tax paid, you received a full deduction for that amount. On that same return, if you were entitled to a state tax refund, then you really deducted more for state tax than you were entitled to. Then when you received the refund the following year, it became taxable. So count it as income if you claimed what is now your tax refund among your itemized deductions in the prior year.

Tax trap!

18 I made a gift of $10,000 to my son. Does he have to pay income tax on this money?

No. Gifts and inheritances are tax-free to the person who receives the gift. The tax law allows you to give up to $10,000 to anyone once a year, tax-free. Contrary to common belief, the gift does not have to be given to a relative, and it can be made to an unlimited number of people. For example, if you had the money, you could make gifts of up to $10,000 each to 100 friends, once a year. The general rule is that the more money you have to give, the more $10,000 gifts you will be able to make, since you will probably have more "friends" and "relatives." A married couple can make annual joint tax-free gifts of up to $20,000 to as many different people as they wish, no matter who writes the check, up to the full $20,000.

If the gift exceeds the $10,000/$20,000 annual limits, there may be a gift tax to pay (see *Question #20*). If there is, the gift tax is paid by the one who has given the gift.

19 If I put my daughter's name on a bank account and make it a joint account for the two of us, do I owe gift tax on that?

No. For bank accounts and for brokerage accounts in which stocks are held in street name ("street name" means the broker holds the certificates for you and provides you with monthly statements), no gift has been made until your daughter actually withdraws the funds. It will not be considered a completed gift for gift tax purposes until that time.

20 I'm single and I gave my friend a gift of $25,000. I know that I have no tax problem with the first $10,000 because I'm allowed to give up to that amount to as many people as I wish once a year. But what are the tax consequences of the remaining $15,000?

First, and most importantly, can I be your friend, too? No? Well then, the answer to this question reflects some of the basics of how the estate and gift tax system works.

The first $10,000, as you correctly stated in your question, has no tax consequences. You can give this amount once a year to as many people as you like, and they need not be relatives. There are no filing requirements with the IRS, and you do not have to disclose such gifts to anyone. If you are married, your spouse can join you in the gift, thus doubling the $10,000 annual limit to $20,000 to each person on whom you bestow a gift or gifts. Gifts may be money, or just about anything else of value, including stock, artwork, or an interest in a home or investment property.

The next $15,000 of your $25,000 gift is over the annual $10,000 limit but is not taxable at this time. This excess cuts into your estate and gift tax exemption, which for 1997 is $600,000. As a result, when you die, your estate will receive $15,000 less of whatever your exemption amount was at death. Under the new tax law, the exemption increases gradually to $1 million in 2006 (see *Question #209* for details). If the exemption is $1 million at your death and you have given no other gifts that would reduce it, then your estate will receive an exemption of $985,000 ($1 million less the $15,000).

All future gifts in excess of the $10,000/$20,000 annual exclusion limits will continue to cut into your exemption until it is used up. Only when and if your estate exemption is exhausted will you be required to pay gift tax.

21 **If I buy U.S. Savings Bonds in my own name, and then later add my child's or grandchild's name to the bond, who pays taxes on the income when it has to be reported?**

You do. Even though you're joint owners, the taxes are paid by the one who actually bought the bond, unless you transfer full ownership to your child or grandchild. If you each paid for half of the bond, you each pay half of the taxes.

22 **My uncle died and I received $500,000 as the beneficiary of his life insurance policy. Is this taxable?**

No. Life insurance proceeds represent tax-free income to beneficiaries.

Good tax law

23 **I'm sick and haven't been able to work for several months. Luckily, I have a good disability policy which is providing me with some income. Are the benefits from the policy taxable?**

It depends on who pays the premiums. If you work for a company that pays disability for you, which is usually the case, you must include your disability income on your taxes. If your employer withholds a portion of the premium from your pay, you can deduct that amount from the amount you report as taxable disability, but this is usually very small.

However, if you pay for your own private disability coverage and become disabled, the disability payments you receive are tax-free.

24. I recently won a suit and received an award for damages. Is this taxable?

It depends when you received it. Under the 1996 tax act, damage awards received after August 20, 1996 are taxable unless they involve physical injury or illness. Payments for emotional distress not attributable to physical injury, discrimination awards, and punitive damages (except for wrongful death) are taxable. (Punitive damages are payments you receive to punish someone else for wrongdoing.) The general rule is if you are going to sue someone for damages, it is not enough that they have called you names—they must also have beaten you up to make any damage awards tax-free. No pain, no gain!

25. I filed to have my property taxes reduced and received a reduction as well as a refund of prior taxes paid. Is this refund taxable?

Generally, yes. Since property taxes or real estate taxes are a deductible item for itemized deduction purposes, you received the benefit of the tax deduction in the year in which you originally paid the tax which has now been refunded. Now that the payment is coming back to you, you must report it as "Other Income" on the front page of your Form 1040. If, however, you did not itemize your deductions and received no tax benefit from them, then you do not have to report such income. You can check IRS Publication 525, "Taxable and Nontaxable Income," which further explains what the IRS calls the "tax benefit rule" to see how much you benefit by this refund and how much of it will be taxable.

26. I have tax-free municipal bonds. Why must I pay tax on the increase in their value between the times I bought and sold them?

While it's true that the interest earned on these bonds is tax-free, when you sell or redeem a bond, the capital gain, if any, is taxable. A gain on the sale of a bond represents appreciation in value and is not the kind of income that is tax-free.

27 **I have stocks I want to sell that would produce huge capital gains. Should I wait until I am in a lower tax bracket to sell them?**

Not necessarily. With the new tax law, the maximum capital gains rate may be either 10% or 20%. This means that even if you're in the highest bracket, say 39.6%, you will pay only 20% tax on your capital gains. (If your bracket goes below 28%, then your capital gains tax rate drops to 10%.) The rule which applies here is: sell when you think it's the right time to sell from an investment point of view. Investment decision-making takes precedence over tax issues.

28 **I've heard that under the new tax law there are more capital gains rates than holes in Sonny Corleone. Could this possibly be explained so I know which rates apply to me?**

Capital gains
"28-25-20-18-10-8, hike!" No, these are not football signals, these are the six new capital gains rates created by the new tax law. That's right, we now have six new rates, and three new time periods for figuring out how your capital gains will be taxed.

New tax law will affect 1997 returns

The maximum tax rate on capital gains has been reduced from 28% to 20%, effective for qualifying sales after May 6, 1997. Here's how capital gains tax will be computed for sales of assets in 1997:

- *For assets sold between January 1 and May 6, 1997, the old rules apply— the maximum capital gains rate of 28% applies on assets held for more than a year* (Gains on short-term sales—those held for one year or less are taxed as regular income.)

- *For assets sold from May 7 through July 28, 1997 the maximum capital gains rate is 20% for assets held for more than one year*

- *From July 29 on, the maximum tax is 20% but assets must be held for more than 18 months* During this period, assets held for more than one year, but not more than 18 months, will be subject to the maximum 28% capital gains rate for this new so-called "midterm period." As before, short-term capital gains (on assets held one year or less) will still be taxed as regular income.

- *For depreciable business real estate assets sold after May 6, 1997, the tax rate is 25% on recapture (see **Questions #110 and #155** for details on recapture)*

As before, if your marginal income tax rate (the rate of tax you pay on your last income) is less than any of the maximum rates above, your capital gains will be added to your income and taxed at the appropriate income tax rate. When and if you cross the threshold to an income tax rate higher than whatever maximum capital gain rate applies, you'll pay the capital gains rate.

There will also be a new lower capital gains rate of 10% for those in the 15% income tax bracket. The new five-year provision going into effect after December 31, 2000 drops the capital gains rate for those in this tax bracket from 10% to 8%. However, in contrast to the requirement for those in higher tax brackets, that the assets be acquired after December 31, 2000, the lower rate is available for assets acquired before the year 2001, but sold after December 31, 2000.

Another new capital gains provision which will kick in with the new millennium: after December 31, 2000, the maximum capital gains rate will drop to 18% for those in higher tax brackets who acquire their assets after this date and hold them for five years. Therefore, the earliest you can get the 18% tax rate is 2006.

Unfortunately, for those who trade in collectibles, the maximum capital gains rate will remain at 28%.

Is this complicated enough? Boy, those guys in Congress are really helping tax book authors!

29 **I have been collecting payments from a property I sold several years ago and have reported the capital gain each year, using the installment sale method. Even though I sold the property before the tax law changed the capital gains rate to 20%, do I qualify for the 20% rate on payments I receive after the law change?**

Yes. The capital gains portion of each payment you receive after May 6, 1997 is eligible for the 20% rate, even though you sold the property several years ago. However, for installment payments received after July 28, 1997, the 20% rate only applies if the property was held for more than 18 months.

30. We just had a huge gain from the sale of a stock. We know that we will owe a lot of money on April 15. Should we increase our estimated tax payments right now to avoid the underpayment penalty?

You will owe the tax, that's true, but you may not have to increase your estimated tax payments if you qualify for an exception to the underpayment penalty. If, by the end of the year, you pay in at least last year's tax, you won't have to increase your estimated tax payments, and as long as you pay all the tax that's due by next April 15, you will not incur a penalty. If your prior year's Adjusted Gross Income exceeded $150,000, however, you must have paid at least 110% of last year's tax to be exempt from the underpayment penalty.

This percentage changes over the next few years before returning to 110% in 2003 as follows:

1998 .... 100%
1999-2001 .... 105%
2002 .... 112%
2003 and later 110%

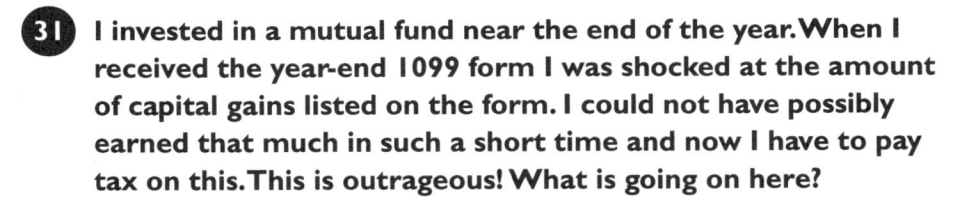

New tax law will affect future returns

31. I invested in a mutual fund near the end of the year. When I received the year-end 1099 form I was shocked at the amount of capital gains listed on the form. I could not have possibly earned that much in such a short time and now I have to pay tax on this. This is outrageous! What is going on here?

A nasty year-end tax trap will catch many mutual fund investors by surprise. It's called the mutual fund tax trap, and it sounds like you got caught.

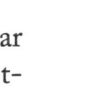

If you're thinking of investing in stock funds near the end of the calendar year, for example, November or December, be careful. Instead of investing, you may be "buying" a tax. It all depends on when you invest.

Tax trap!

First...the basics
Mutual funds are entities set up as conduits that pool investors' money and pass income and capital gains back to those investors. By law, funds

must distribute at least 90% of their income to investors on an annual basis. Distributions of income may be made as dividends (taxed as ordinary income) or as capital gains.

Record date
The "record date" (usually in early December) is the date the mutual fund uses to determine whether shareholders will receive a distribution. For example, if a fund announces a record date of December 5, 1997, then shareholders "of record"—those who own shares on that date—will receive the distribution. Anyone investing after that date will not.

Year-end mutual funds purchases may incur unwanted capital gains

Tax trap!

It might seem at first blush that a good investment strategy would be to make your investment just before the record date so that you could qualify for the capital gain or dividend distribution. This is a classic tax trap and should be avoided. Here's why. Let's say you've invested $20,000 in a fund by purchasing 2,000 shares at $10 per share. After you invest, the fund declares an income distribution of $2 per share. The fund's share value then automatically drops by the amount of the distribution, in this case, $2. The value of your investment after the distribution is then $8 per share ($10 less $2) or $16,000, not the $20,000 you had originally invested. You will owe taxes on the $4,000 distribution, which is really nothing more than a tax on your own money. If you reinvest your distributions you will recoup this loss when you sell your shares because you will increase your basis (your cost, which you must exceed before further tax will be owed) in the fund by $4,000, the amount of the distribution.

Taking the example above, suppose you had decided not to reinvest distributions and you sold all your 2000 shares at $8—the price of the shares after the distribution noted—for a total of $16,000. Since your cost basis—the amount you had originally paid—was $20,000, you would have a loss of $4,000, which would offset the phantom income that you had already paid tax on. The problem is that if you want to hold on to your shares for the long term, you will be out the tax that you paid up front on the distribution until the day you sell. Remember: even if you did not actually receive the income distribution declared in 1997 until sometime in 1998, it is still taxable in 1997 if you were a shareholder on the record date in 1997.

If you're considering investing in a mutual fund at year-end, first call the fund and find out when the record date is, and then invest after that date. However, this tax problem does not to apply to mutual fund investments in an IRA, annuity, or other retirement account, because earnings on these accounts are tax-deferred.

Reverse strategy

If you're considering selling your shares, use the reverse strategy and sell before the record date. Here, you save taxes by turning ordinary income into capital gains.

Reinvestment of income and capital gains

Remember: even if you elect to reinvest your dividends and/or capital gains distributions to buy new shares from the mutual fund, they are still as fully taxable as if you had received a check for the full amount.

32 Are executor's fees taxable as my personal income?

Yes. And so are trustee's fees.

This is the reason why you should not automatically accept an executor's fee, especially if you're the sole beneficiary of an estate valued at less than $600,000 for 1997. The estate and gift tax exemption increases gradually to $1 million in 2006 (see *Question #209*) and if you take the money as a beneficiary through inheritance from an estate which is under the exemption instead of as an executor, it will be tax-free to you.

If, on the other hand, the estate is a taxable estate valued at over $600,000 in 1997, then it might pay to take the fee, because the fee would become a deduction on the estate tax return. Although it would still be income to you as executor, your income tax rate would likely be lower than the estate tax rate. The larger the estate, the more advantageous it is to take the executor's fee.

If you're not a beneficiary it also pays to take the fee since giving it up means that you lose it, and that would be foolish, unless you were just a really nice person.

Executors' and trustees' fees are not subject to the self-employment tax, unless the executor or trustee is a professional, i.e., in the business of being a fiduciary, such as a trust company or an attorney who performs these services as a business.

33 I sold some stock that I inherited from my grandfather. What do I use for my cost in figuring gain or loss?

Inherited property receives favorable income tax treatment. Your cost—or "basis"— is stepped up to the estate tax value, meaning that you're relieved of paying income tax on any appreciation in value from the day your grandfather acquired the stock to the date of his death.

Example:
Your grandfather buys 1,000 shares of stock in 1940 at $10 per share for a cost of $10,000.

Value of the stock at the date of your grandfather's death $500,000
You sell the stock for $500,000
The taxable gain is zero because you get to raise your basis from the original cost of $10,000 to the estate tax value of $500,000. Since you sold the stock for the same $500,000 as your basis, you keep the $500,000—no income tax!

If you had sold the stock for $600,000, you would have had to pay capital gains tax on only the $100,000 increase in value since the date of death, and it would be treated as a long-term capital gain even if the stock had been held for less than one year.

Why is the government so generous with this step-up in basis rule? What's the catch?

The catch is the estate tax. Property that is stepped up in the manner just described is subject to estate tax before the proceeds are inherited. The federal estate tax rates start at 37% and can reach over 50%, considerably higher than the 20% maximum capital gains rate. Congress up to now has chosen not to hit you for both the estate and income tax: they've simply chosen the higher estate tax.

If you were given the stock instead of inheriting it, see the next question.

34 **I sold some stock that my grandfather had given me. What do I use for my cost in figuring gain or loss?**

The rule here is much different from the one that was outlined above for stock inherited from your grandfather. When you sell property you received as a gift, it does not receive a step-up in basis. So let's say we change our example in *Question #33* to your having received the stock as a gift from your grandfather while he was still alive. If you sold the stock for $500,000, you would pay capital gains tax on a gain of $490,000 (the $500,000 selling price, less your grandfather's original cost of $10,000).

Tax trap!

Section 4
Your Tax Deduction Questions

If you haven't any charity in your heart, you have the worst kind of heart trouble.

  Bob Hope

Everyone wants tax deductions—some people will do almost anything to get them. Yet, as eager as most folks are to claim these nuggets, the biggest ones are the ones most often overlooked. That's why I'm starting off here with "The Five Most Overlooked Tax Deductions."

On the other hand, there are a whole bunch of items that may not be as deductible as you have been told by the authorities at the club, or at the mahjongg or canasta tables, where "tax experts" often dispense free (which is about what it's worth) advice.

Either way, I'll answer your most pressing questions about this all-important area…

35 What are the most overlooked tax deductions?

High taxes are bad enough, but paying more than you have to is even worse. Here are the five deductions that are most often missed by hardworking taxpayers:

Reinvested dividends

It's a common practice to reinvest mutual fund or stock dividends instead of collecting them in cash. However, when investors sell, they may forget to deduct those reinvested dividends from their gain or to add them to their loss. Since tax was already paid on the reinvested dividends in the year in which they were received, the dividends should be added to the cost of the stock when figuring gain or loss on the sale of the stock. If you fail to take this into account, it means you will pay tax twice on the same stock sale: once when the dividend was first reinvested, and again when the stock is sold. To make sure that you take credit for all reinvested dividends, go back to prior tax returns or keep a separate record. Remember to keep all year-end mutual fund statements.

Hot tip!

Points on refinanced mortgages

If you paid points on refinancing, you generally cannot take a full deduction in the year you paid the points (in contrast to the first mortgage, on which points are fully deductible in the year they are paid). Instead, the IRS requires that the points be deducted over the life of the refinanced loan (the financial term for this is "amortization"). However, if you have refinanced a refinanced loan (in other words, refinanced for a second time) *all* the remaining points that have not been deducted on the first refinance can now be deducted, since that loan has now been paid off.

Prior years' state tax paid

If you itemize your deductions, you're entitled to deduct on your federal return any state tax you've paid for the current year or any state tax you may have owed for prior years that were paid during the year. Beware: interest and penalties on unpaid tax are not deductible. Look at last year's state return to see if you owed.

State tax breaks

Many states have their own unique tax breaks, but it's not always easy to take advantage of them. This is because most states' returns use the federal tax return as a starting point and you have to adjust your state return to gain the tax breaks. Most of these tax breaks deal with exclusions for certain types of pension income, homeowner or renter tax credits, U.S. government bond interest (taxable on the federal but not on state returns) and Social Security benefits, which most states do not tax.

Loss carryovers

Look back at last year's taxes for loss carryovers. These are losses incurred in prior years which could not be deducted in those years due to loss limitations. They're not permanently lost, but can be used in future years. Losses may be capital losses from stock and property sales or business losses known as "net operating losses." There are also losses from sales of property or equipment used in a trade or business, known in tax talk as "ordinary" losses (as opposed to the capital losses mentioned above). Capital losses are netted first against capital gains and are then deductible against ordinary income up to $3,000 per year. Unused losses are carried forward indefinitely to future years until used up, but upon death, if the losses cannot be used on the final tax return, they expire. The estate itself cannot use the carryover.

36. What tax deductions are available when you refinance a home mortgage?

The main deductions are mortgage interest expense and points, but you must itemize your deductions in order to take them, unless the refinance is on a business or rental property. Here is how it works:

Deducting interest and points on refinancing
Figuring out the tax deductions for interest and points on that refinanced mortgage is no easy task.

On a simple refinancing where you replace your old mortgage with a new mortgage for the amount currently owed, the interest is fully deductible, as long as the interest on the old mortgage was deductible. For example, say in 1979 you purchased a home for $200,000, taking a 20-year 12% mortgage for $150,000. In 1997, your mortgage balance is $100,000. You now refinance for 15 years at 7%. If you refinance for $100,000, which is the same amount as the existing mortgage just before the refinancing, the interest will be fully deductible.

Now let's take another example using the first example as a starting point. Assume that at the time of refinancing in 1997, the house is worth $350,000, and you decide to refinance for $300,000. The first $100,000 goes to pay off the balance on the first mortgage, and the interest on this portion is fully deductible. Let's say the next $150,000 goes as a deposit on a second home. The interest here will also be fully deductible if the loan is secured by the second home. Now suppose the next $20,000 is paid to a contractor to remodel the second home. Yes, the interest on this portion is also fully deductible, because it qualifies as debt used to acquire or substantially improve the first or second home. You now have $30,000 left, which is used to pay off credit card debt and other miscellaneous nondeductible personal expenses. The interest expense on the final $30,000 is also fully deductible as home equity debt, even if it is used to pay nondeductible expenses.

This sounds great, but there are limits. In general, interest on debts incurred to acquire, construct, or substantially improve a main or second home is fully deductible on a mortgage amount of up to $1 million ($500,000 for each partner if married filing separately). In addition, interest on $100,000 ($50,000 each if married filing separately) of mortgage debt is fully deductible as home equity debt, even when used, as in the example above, to pay off credit card debt and other miscellaneous nondeductible personal expenses. Altogether, interest is fully deductible on up to $1.1 million of debt.

Deducting points paid on refinancing

If you paid points on refinancing, you will generally not receive a full deduction in the year the points were paid. Instead, the IRS requires that the points be deducted over the life of the refinanced loan (as mentioned previously, the financial term for this is "amortization"). For example, if you paid $2,000 in points on a 20-year mortgage, the deduction will be $100 per year for 20 years. Also, if part of the refinanced mortgage is used for home improvements, that portion of the points paid is deductible in the year paid and the remainder is deducted over the life of the loan. For example, if you paid $2,000 in points on a 20-year refinance for $100,000, and used $30,000 for home improvements, then 30% ($30,000 divided by $100,000) of the $2,000 in points paid, or $600, would be currently deductible, and the remaining $1,400 of points would be amortized over the 20-year loan term.

The rules for deducting points on refinanced loans differ from points paid to purchase or improve your principal residence, which can be deducted in full in the year paid, as long as the loan is secured by your principal residence and the points are actually paid.

Don't miss this deduction

One final tip: if you refinance a refinanced loan (in other words, refinance for a second time), all the remaining points that have not been deducted on the first refinance can be deducted in the year of the refinance. This is the most commonly overlooked tax deduction on a refinancing.

37 **I don't show enough income to support my mortgage interest deductions. Should I exclude the deductions from my return?**

Tax trap!

You have bigger problems. The IRS already knows about your mortgage interest because that's been reported directly to the IRS by the bank. And, based on where you live, the IRS probably has a good idea of how much you pay in real estate taxes as well. Since, the IRS already has all this information, whether or not you claim the deductions, your return may trigger one of the new "economic reality" or "lifestyle" audits. When deductions that the IRS already knows about exceed the income you're showing on the return, you're asking for trouble, unless you can show some other source of income, such as an inheritance or gifts. Of course, this being the IRS, you'll have to be able to prove it.

38. My car was stolen and I have a huge loss. But I do not want to report it to the insurance company because my rates will go sky high. Am I entitled to deduct the loss as a theft loss on my tax return?

No. The government will not act as a partial insurer. This rule holds true for all casualty and theft losses. If you're covered by insurance and you do not make the claim, you cannot take the loss. But the deduction may not be as much as you think because, to be deductible, the loss must exceed 10% of your Adjusted Gross Income. There is a $100 deductible for each loss in addition to the limit.

39. Can anything be done to offset the income tax I'm supposed to pay on my unemployment benefits?

Yes. Although you cannot reduce the gross amount of benefits you must report, if you're unemployed and are looking for work, you may be able to deduct job hunting expenses if you itemize your deductions.

Job hunting expenses include all sorts of great items, such as travel to interviews, long distance phone calls, typing of résumés, the cost of printing and mailing résumés, maintaining or assembling a portfolio, and career counseling in certain cases where it might maintain or increase your skills in your chosen field. Also, any fees you may pay to professionals to review employment contracts are deductible, as is placing an ad in a newspaper. Job hunting expenses are deductible only as itemized deductions, and must exceed 2% of Adjusted Gross Income (AGI) to be deductible. If you have to go out of town, the cost of that trip (only the business part, not the personal part) is deductible, including travel expenses, meals (limited to 50%), lodging, and local transportation. If you have to buy certain publications or trade magazines to keep up with the latest trends, or find out where the jobs are, that is also deductible. Remember: you must keep records!

Job hunting expenses are not deductible if you're looking for a job that is outside your current line of business. Let's say you're a computer analyst and you were just laid off. If you decide you want to be a lawyer, the cost of looking for a job in the legal field is not deductible.

40 Can I still deduct job hunting expenses if I don't find a job by the end of the year?

Yes.

41 My employer has required that I take certain courses to maintain and improve my skills, but he won't pay for them. Can I deduct these costs?

Generally, yes, but there are some tax rules to follow.

'97 New tax law will affect 1997 returns

If you can get your employer to crack open his piggy bank, the new tax law extends the tax break for employer-provided educational assistance. Under the previous law, which expired after June 30, 1997, you were able to receive up to $5,250 of educational assistance from your employer, tax-free. The new tax law extends this benefit to courses beginning before June 1, 2000 but applies only to undergraduate education. (The exclusion for graduate level courses expired June 30, 1996.) See the questions below for more information on tax relief for workers taking courses to improve their skills.

To get the deduction, you must pass the tests

To get a deduction on education that you paid for, it must be required by your employer, or it must maintain or improve your current job skills. Even if you meet one of the requirements, if the education you receive earns you a degree that qualifies you for a new occupation or profession, the expenses are not deductible, even if you choose not to work in the field for which you have newly qualified.

For example, if you're working as an accountant and attending law school at night, you will not be allowed a deduction for the law school costs, even if you never intend to practice law. The tax reasoning behind this is that law school has qualified you for a new profession. There is, however, an exception for certain teachers who are required as a job condition to take courses that may lead to a degree.

You're also not entitled to education deductions if you're a student taking courses that will prepare you for your first job in your field. For example, if you enrolled in a secretarial school, then went on to your first position as a secretary, the school costs would not be deductible because the courses enabled you to begin your career in the secretarial field. If, on the other hand, you were already employed as a secretary, and you took the courses to improve your typing skills, the deduction would be allowed.

What you can deduct

If your education qualifies under the rules mentioned above, you can deduct tuition, books, supplies, and related expenses. Expenses allowed include school and computer supplies, lab fees, typing, writing, and research expenses. Also included are certain auto, travel, and meal expenses. Normally the costs of commuting are not deductible, but if you work during the day and go to school at night, the costs associated with your trip from work to school are deductible. If you attend courses or seminars away from home, the transportation, meals (limited to 50%), and lodging expenses are deductible, in addition to the actual cost of the seminar itself. Employees must itemize in order to take education deductions. You claim these along with your other miscellaneous itemized deductions, the total of which must exceed 2% of your Adjusted Gross Income to be deductible.

Self-employed folks deduct the expenses on Schedule C (not reduced by the 2% of AGI). Remember to document all your expenses.

42 What are the new education tax breaks which will be available beginning in 1998?

The four tax-breaks outlined below are the HOPE Scholarship Tax Credit, the Lifetime Learning Credit, the Education IRA, and new deductions on interest paid on student loans. *Beware: for any eligible child you may use only one of the first three.*

HOPE Scholarship Tax Credit

Effective in 1998, a $1,500 tax credit is available for tuition, fees, and related college expenses (but not room and board and books) for the first two years of school. The credit is based on 100% of the first $1,000 of qualified expenses and 50% of the next $1,000. Phaseout begins at $80,000 for couples and $40,000 for individuals. If you are convicted of federal or

New tax law will affect future returns

state drug charges, you are specifically excluded from claiming the Hope Credit but not the Lifetime Learning Credit. So, if you are on drugs, I recommend the Lifetime Learning Credit.

Lifetime Learning Credit
This is a separate tax credit for tuition and fees paid after June 30, 1998 for college or graduate school. (For most people, the HOPE Scholarship is better for the first two years of college, because it gives the bigger tax credit.) It's also available to workers who take courses to maintain or improve their job skills. The amount of the credit is a maximum of $1,000—20% of up to $5,000 of tuition expenses (beginning in 2002, the maximum credit increases to 20% of $10,000 of qualified expenses). Phase-out begins at $80,000 for couples and $40,000 for individuals.

Education IRAs
Beginning in 1998, you can contribute up to $500 to a nondeductible IRA for each child less than 18 years old. Withdrawals used for education will be tax-free. Eligibility for the education IRA begins to phase out when income hits $95,000 for singles and $150,000 for couples. All money must be withdrawn by the time the child turns 30 years of age, and if not used for education expenses, it is subject to a 10% penalty.

The education IRA may be tapped for either undergraduate or graduate courses, and, like the HOPE and Lifetime Learning Credits, can be used for tuition, fees, and related college expenses. Unlike the Hope and Lifetime Learning Credits, funds withdrawn from an education IRA can also be used for room and board, and books. *Beware:* we do not know yet, but it appears likely that saving for education with an education IRA may affect schools' assessments of your financial need, hence your child's access to financial aid.

You may also make penalty, and in some circumstances tax-free, withdrawals from your other IRAs for the purpose of educating your children. These opportunities are covered in detail in ***Questions #171-#173***.

Deductions for student loan interest
Beginning in 1998, interest paid by students, and parents of students, on student loans will be deductible, increasing from $1,000 in 1998 up to $2,500 in 2001.

Year   Deduction limited to
1998 .... $1,000
1999 1,500
2000 2,000
2001 2,500

Student loan interest is an "above the line" deduction, meaning it is not an itemized deduction and is not subject to any Adjusted Gross Income (AGI) limitations. Rather, this deduction reduces AGI. You can use it even if you do not itemize. The deduction begins to phase out at $60,000 of income for couples and $40,000 for individuals. Interest is only deductible for the first five years of the loan repayment period. However, if there is a period of interest deferral, it won't count toward the five-year limit. You cannot take the deduction if you can be claimed as a dependent on another person's return, such as your parents. But you can take the deduction if you are a parent who is paying a student loan for a child whom you claim as a dependent.

43 Which of the two tax breaks—HOPE or Lifetime Learning Credit—should I use for my child who is going to college this fall?

In any year, and for any individual, you must choose one of the following three: the Education IRA, the Hope Tax Credit, or the Lifetime Learning Credit. For example, you can use the HOPE Scholarship Tax Credit for one child and the Lifetime Learning Credit for another, but you cannot use both for any single child.

New tax law will affect future returns

The HOPE Scholarship Tax Credit is calculated for each individual. If you have two children, both who qualify, you may claim up to a $3,000 tax credit (up to $1,500 for each child).

The Lifetime Learning Credit is, on the other hand, a per return credit. Therefore, even if you have three children who qualify, you are still limited to a maximum credit of $1,000 on your tax return (20% of up to $5,000 in education expenses).

If you must choose between tax breaks, the HOPE Credit may be the better option if you have more than one child and enough education expenses to claim the $1,500 maximum credit for each child. Remember, the HOPE Credit is limited to the first two years of college and cannot include graduate or advanced degree programs, whereas the Lifetime Learning Credit is available for an unlimited number of years of college, graduate, professional degree, or non-college courses taken by workers to maintain or improve current job skills. The Lifetime Learning Credit is also available for the first two years of college. My real "HOPE" is that you don't have to go to college just to understand how these complicated tax provisions work.

If you are the parent of a student, the HOPE or Lifetime Learning credits are available to you only if your child is your dependent. A student cannot claim the credits on their own return if they are claimed on the parents' return.

44 I heard about the new law allowing interest deductions on student loans. I am now repaying an old student loan. Can I now deduct this interest?

New tax law will affect future returns

Beginning in 1998, you can deduct your old student loan interest up to the new yearly limits, if your loan is less than five years old.

45 My spouse and I have a child in college. We plan to file married-separate because the tax came out slightly lower that way. Who claims the education credits?

Nobody. Parents must file a joint return to claim the education credits.

46 If I contribute $500 to an Education IRA for my child, can I still contribute the full $2,000 to my traditional (or new Roth) IRA?

New tax law will affect future returns

Yes. Although it's called an Education "IRA," it's not considered an IRA for IRA limit purposes and does not affect the amount of your regular IRA contribution. Don't ask me why they call it an IRA when it really isn't one (see Question #42 for additional information on this point).

47 **I took out a student loan to pay for tuition. Do I qualify for either of the education tax credits even though I used the loan to pay my tuition?**

Yes. Under a special provision in the new tax law, tuition and fees paid with loan proceeds are eligible for the Lifetime Learning (but not the HOPE) credit, as long as you qualify under the other requirements. This means that you can receive a credit with no out-of-pocket cost, since the tuition is being paid from the loan proceeds. Plus, when you repay the loan you may be eligible for the new deduction for interest on student loans (see *Question #42*). Remember, all of this does not go into effect until 1998.

Good tax law

48 **I am repaying a student loan. Do these repayments qualify me for the HOPE or Lifetime Learning Credit tax credits?**

No. Now you're pushing it! But you may qualify for the deduction of interest on student loans.

49 **I still owe the college for 1997 tuition for my son. In 1998 I will be able to pay the 1997 past due tuition in full. Am I entitled to any of the new education tax credits?**

No. Although you paid the bill in 1998, in order to qualify for either the Hope tax credit or the Lifetime Learning Credit, the tuition must be paid for 1998 courses or semesters.

50 **The education tax credits you discussed in Questions #42-#47 are great, but they only go so far. Do you know any other tax breaks to help finance my child's education?**

Yes, here are a few ideas:

Using home equity
You can deduct the interest on home equity debt up to $100,000, no matter how you use the proceeds. If you use the home equity loan in lieu of, or in addition to, a student loan, the interest will be deductible. Be careful: you could lose your home if the loan is not repaid.

Estate and gift tax savings

If you have a wealthy relative or friend who wants to help with the bills, there are estate and gift tax advantages available to that wonderful saint. She or he may give $10,000 ($20,000 for joint gifts) once a year to as many people as they like, tax free.

In addition, they can make unlimited, but nondeductible, gifts to benefit your son or daughter as long as the check is made out directly to the college or institution. This exclusion applies only to tuition. The gift of education is a wonderful and productive way to reduce estate taxes if you or your child would have been the eventual beneficiary anyway.

51 I gave gifts of $10,000 to each of my two children. Can I deduct this?

No. If they allowed you to receive tax deductions for gifts you make to people, we would have a country filled with obscenely generous people. Hey…wait a minute…that doesn't sound so bad!

You only receive a tax deduction for gifts to charities, not to individuals. The tax break here is that you get to remove the money from your estate, without paying gift tax, for annual gifts of $10,000 or less per person.

P.S. For those who try to claim that their children are charity cases, forget it. That's their problem, not the IRS's.

52 Should I give my son a mortgage so he can buy a home? And if I do, can my son deduct the mortgage interest he pays me?

When dealing with relatives, the loan must be what the IRS calls an "arm's length transaction," which means it has to be at fair market interest rates backed by collateral and guarantees, and it has to be a bona fide loan (not some arrangement set up to look like a loan). For your son to take a deduction for mortgage interest paid, the loan must be secured by the newly-purchased home, which means the mortgage must be recorded (filed at your county clerk's office as an official mortgage). Are you willing to do this? If you are, then your son may deduct the mortgage interest.

If your son doesn't repay you, the IRS just might call this a gift, subjecting you to gift taxes for any amount over $10,000 in one year—or $20,000 if you're married. Above the $10,000 or $20,000 gift limits, the amount of this "gift" cuts into your estate and gift tax exemption amount of $600,000 for 1997. Worse case scenario? You can look at this as early estate planning—your son got part of his inheritance while you are still alive.

My experience has taught me to advise my clients to ask themselves a simple question before they loan money to anyone, especially a close family member, "How far am I willing to go to enforce this loan if they cannot pay?"

53 Our family gave a ton of clothing and lots of household items to a charitable organization. Over the years these items probably cost us over $20,000. How much can we deduct?

Not $20,000, not even close.

Generally, you can deduct the fair market value on the date of the gift. The fact that you paid $20,000 for the property will have no effect on what the property is actually worth on the date of the donation.

Often people are shocked to find out that their "priceless" family heirlooms and used designer clothing are worth pennies on the dollar to the IRS. There is no "official" price guide on gifts of property, but the IRS often uses thrift shop values or values used by local charities, who sometimes publish lists. You may have a sweater that cost you over $100, but as a tax deduction after only a year of use, it may only be worth $10 to $15. When I prepare returns, some people go through long stories to convince me of the true intrinsic value that "you just can't see on the surface," but their stories won't hold up with our friends at the IRS.

The IRS, in its Publication 526, "Charitable Contributions," states that "the fair market value of used clothing and other personal items is usually far less than the price you paid for them." This should give you an idea of how they will value your precious used items.

If the tax deduction value you place on your donated property exceeds $500, you must fill out Form 8283, "Noncash Charitable Contributions," and attach it to your return. This is probably why we see so many items valued at $499.

In addition, if you claim a deduction for a single item or a similar group of items worth over $5,000, you must add to the above requirements a qualified written appraisal from a qualified appraiser. Obviously, when you get to this point, it must be the real thing.

54. I donated blood to the Red Cross. Can I get a tax deduction for this?

No. Even donating your lifeblood is not enough to gain a tax deduction from the IRS!

55. While I am out doing volunteer work for my church, I have to pay a baby sitter to watch my children. Is this deductible?

No.

56. Can I get a deduction for the value of my time or the services that I donate to charitable organizations?

No. But you can take a deduction for unreimbursed out-of-pocket expenses, like supplies you bought for the group, coffee or food for charity functions, or items such as awards, which you bought for a religious, educational, or other charitable group affair or meeting. You cannot take a deduction for personal, living or family expenses.

You can also deduct auto expenses that are directly related to your volunteer work. You can use 12 cents a mile (in 1998 it goes up to 14 cents) or your actual auto expenses, plus parking and tolls, as long as it is directly related to a qualifying charitable organization. A qualified charity is one that is registered with the IRS.

57. How do I know if an organization is a "qualified" charity and registered with the IRS?

You can go to your local library and look them up in IRS Publication 78, "Cumulative List of Organizations," which lists most qualified organizations and is regularly updated. Recognized religious organizations do not have to apply. This information is also available at the IRS site at *http://www.irs.ustreas.gov* on the internet. You can also call the IRS toll-free in your area.

58 What are all these year-end forms I am receiving from organizations I donated money to during the year? Is this something new?

Yes. This started in 1994. Here are the rules.

SUBSTANTIATION REQUIREMENTS FOR CLAIMING CHARITABLE DEDUCTIONS
The $250 rule

You need more than canceled checks to substantiate certain contributions and/or gifts.

In order for a charitable contribution of $250 or more to be considered an acceptable tax deduction, you must obtain from the charity written substantiation (a receipt or statement), which reports the amount of the contribution, the value of any goods or services received in exchange for the contribution (such as a dinner or a gift), and (in the case of a noncash contribution) a description of the donated property.

Separate payments generally will be treated as separate contributions, and do not have to be combined in order to reach the $250 threshold, even if in total they exceed $250. So, if you made five separate donations of $200 each on five different days, the $250 substantiation rules do not apply, even though your total contribution to the organization is in excess of $250. This seems like a nice loophole. I probably should not have mentioned it. Don't tell the IRS about this, OK?

Good tax law

The $75 rule

When a contribution is in excess of $75, but you receive goods and services in return, the charity must provide you with a good faith estimate of the value of the goods and services you received, in order to keep you from claiming that portion as a charitable contribution.

Let's say you pay $100 to the charity to attend a special dinner event. If the dinner is worth $40, then your actual deduction is limited to $60. The charity must provide you with a statement giving you their estimate of the value of the dinner.

However, this can get tricky. Let's say you pay $10,000 to a charity for the privilege of having dinner with Barbara Streisand. It's going to be tough for the charity to put a value on the amount of time Barbara Streisand has spent with you, but this has to be done in order to figure out the actual net value of the deductible contribution.

So the taxpayer will not shoulder the extra burden that accompanies the requirements affecting charitable donations. The charitable organizations have to comply or be subject to fines. See, now even charities can get penalties. You're not alone.

59 How much can I deduct for contributions?

As much as you want.

I love this question! There is no "magic" maximum amount that you can deduct for charitable contributions.

There is a limitation, but it rarely comes into effect for cash contributions, you can only deduct up to one-half of your Adjusted Gross Income (AGI) in a given year. Any excess, however, can be carried over to the following year or years. For contributions of capital gain property, such as stock, you're limited to 30% of your AGI.

60 Can I deduct the cost of long-term care insurance?

Yes. Beginning in 1997, limited medical deductions will be allowed to help cover the cost of long-term care insurance. Long-term care consists of any assistance or supervision required for daily essential activities of life, such as bathing, eating, dressing, or moving about. Long-term care insurance covers the cost of hiring a care-giver, nurse, or layperson who assists in any of these activities. Such care may be given at home or at an adult home, a nursing home, or a skilled nursing facility. The amount that can be deducted is limited, based on age as follows:

Age (as of the end of the tax year) limitation:
Under age 41 .... $200
Age 41-50 .... $375
Age 51-60 .... $750
Age 61-70 .... $2,000
Over age 70 .... $2,500

The limit is per person, not per return. For example, for a married couple, each of whom is over age 70, the limit is $2,500 each—or a total of $5,000—if they each have eligible policies.

In addition to the limitations stated above, you must itemize to get the deduction, since it can only be claimed as a medical deduction. To be deductible, long term care premiums, combined with all other medical expenses, must exceed 7.5% of your Adjusted Gross Income.

Policies issued before 1996 automatically qualify, but those issued later must meet certain technical requirements to qualify.

New 1099-LTC forms for long term care benefits

Beginning in January 1998, insurance companies will be required to send out a new 1099-LTC to those who received benefits in the previous year. The 1099-LTC will state the amount received and whether the benefits were paid from a qualified or non-qualified insurance plan. Benefits of up to $175 per day (or the amount of qualified long term care expenses incurred, if higher) are not taxable if paid from a qualified long term care policy. Even if you think that you will receive no benefit from the medical deduction for long term care premiums (because you do not itemize or will not reach the 7.5% threshold), you should still purchase only qualified policies because you will have to pay tax on any benefits accrued from non-qualified policies.

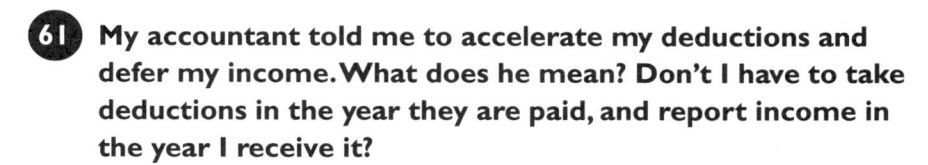

New tax law will affect future returns

61 **My accountant told me to accelerate my deductions and defer my income. What does he mean? Don't I have to take deductions in the year they are paid, and report income in the year I receive it?**

Yes. But the strategy here is to time these items to best fit your tax situation. Here are some examples of how to accelerate and defer to your advantage:

Accelerate itemized deductions

Medical expenses and some miscellaneous itemized deductions are allowable only to the extent that they exceed certain percentage limitations. For medical expenses to be deductible, they must exceed 7.5% of Adjusted Gross Income (AGI). If you do not have enough expenses to exceed the 7.5% limitation, consider prepaying some of next year's medi-

Hot tip!

cal bills. By bunching two years' expenses into one year, you may be able to create a tax deduction. The same theory works for miscellaneous itemized deductions, which are subject to a 2% limitation before they become deductible.

An alternative strategy is to delay payment of this year's expenses until next year. Then you can bunch them with other expenses next year and gain a tax deduction next year, as opposed to coming up short and losing a tax deduction for both years. The correlation to this strategy on the charitable donation side is to make all planned contributions this year. You can charge your contributions on a credit card and get the deduction for this year even if you do not pay the credit card bill until next year.

Defer income to next year

A parallel strategy is to delay income, for example, electing to delay a bonus or self-employment income to next year. This will reduce this year's income, and could also increase your effective itemized deductions, since they must exceed a percentage of your AGI. This combination of lower income and higher deductions can mean real tax savings.

62 I finally did some estate planning. Is the cost of preparing a will and trust deductible?

No. However, if there is an allocation on the bill from your attorney for the portion of fees that can be related to tax advice, that amount is deductible as a miscellaneous itemized deduction, subject to the 2% of Adjusted Gross Income limit. Ask your attorney for an itemized invoice.

63 I think my accountant made a mistake on my return on Schedule A, "Itemized Deductions." The deductions add up to $32,000, but his total shows $31,038. What happened?

Tax law. Leave it up to the government to create a form that doesn't add up. You were probably subject to the 3% overall deductions limit on itemized deductions. In 1997, if married and filing joint, this reduction of deductions begins when your Adjusted Gross Income (AGI) reaches $121,200. What this means is that if your AGI is greater than $121,200, you begin to lose your itemized deductions to the extent of 3% of the amount of your AGI that is over the limit.

For example, if your AGI is $150,000, and your itemized deductions add up to $32,000, you will lose $864 of deductions because your AGI exceeds the $121,200 limit by $28,800 ($150,000 less $121,200), and 3% of that excess $28,800 equals $864. That's why your Schedule A appears to be added incorrectly by $864.

This tax form actually does not add up to itself because that's the way the geniuses who sit around in Washington dreaming up tax code decided to do it. And guess what? The rest of us will all have to live with it...

64 What happened to my miscellaneous itemized deductions? I know I had some work-related expenses and my tax preparation fees were included, but I received no deduction. Why?

Welcome to the 2% limit on miscellaneous itemized deductions! Most miscellaneous itemized deductions are subject to a reduction by the amount equal to 2% of your Adjusted Gross Income (AGI). For example, if a married couple has joint AGI of $80,000, the miscellaneous itemized deductions must exceed $1,600 ($80,000 x the 2% of AGI limit). This 2% limitation applies only to the miscellaneous itemized deductions and has nothing to do with the 3% overall itemized deduction limitation which applies only to certain higher income taxpayers. (See *Question #63* for more information on this.)

Examples of items that could be limited by the 2% rule are all work-related expenses, such as educational expenses, job hunting expenses, tax preparation fees, safe deposit box fees, costs of uniforms, and other job-related equipment and supplies.

To answer your question, your AGI was high enough to wipe out all of your miscellaneous itemized deductions. That's why you didn't see it on your return. Tax preparers will often leave the section blank rather than list tax deductions they know you won't get.

65 Are there any miscellaneous itemized deductions that are not subject to the 2% limit?

Very few, and those usually have their own limitations. For example, gambling and lottery losses are not limited to the 2%, but they are limited to the extent of winnings. One interesting deduction, the 691(c) deduction for estate tax, is not subject to the 2% limit. This is the deduction for estate tax attributable to an item of Income in Respect of a Decedent (IRD), a potentially large but obscure deduction (see *Question #196* for more details).

66 How much can I get for my kids?

I know the feeling, but I think you may be asking about the new Child Tax Credit.

Child tax credits

Beginning in 1998, a $400 tax credit is available to parents for each child under 17 years of age, increasing to $500 in 1999. The credit will phase out as income exceeds $75,000 (single or head of household) or $110,000 (married).

New tax law will affect future returns

67 What happened to the tax deductions for my children? My accountant must have made a mistake on my return.

For those of you who think of your children as little tax deductions, think again. For certain higher income taxpayers, those little tax deductions may be worth little, or may even be phased out!

For filing 1997 tax returns, the new personal exemption deduction amount is $2,650 for each exemption claimed. For families with dependent children, this may be a sizable deduction. For example, a family of five (husband, wife, and three children) receives a personal exemption deduction of $13,250 (five exemptions of $2,650 each). However, when Adjusted Gross Income (AGI) exceeds $181,800 (for 1997), your deduction begins to be reduced, and when it reaches $304,300 your deduction is lost, or in tax talk, "phased out."

Under these complicated rules, for each increment of $2,500 that your AGI exceeds $181,800, (if you're married filing jointly), you lose 2% of all your exemptions.

Example #1:

If your AGI exceeded the $181,800 by $100,000, you will lose 80% of personal exemptions ($100,000 divided by $2,500 equals 40, and 40 multiplied by 2 equals 80%).

Example #2:

For a more complicated situation, let's say you're married with three dependent children, and your AGI is $200,000. Your personal exemptions will be reduced by 16%, which is $2,120 out of the original total of $13,250 in exemptions.

Here's how it's figured: As AGI exceeds the threshold amount of $181,800, the personal exemptions begin to phase out. The excess of $18,200 ($200,000 less $181,800) is then divided by $2,500, which equals 7.28. Rounded to the next highest number this becomes 8 (yes, the IRS rounds *up*). The 8 is then multiplied by 2%, making the loss 16% of personal exemptions. The personal exemption deduction of $13,250 is therefore reduced by $2,120 ($13,250 multiplied by 16%), netting your family a deduction of $11,130.

As a result of this reduction calculation, any time AGI exceeds the threshold amount by $122,500, personal exemptions will be totally lost. If you file married filing jointly, your exemptions will be fully phased out when AGI exceeds $304,300 ($181,800 plus $122,500 equals $304,300). For single individuals, the 1997 threshold amount is $121,200; for heads of household, $151,500; and for married filing separately, $90,900.

68 Do the new tax laws help parents who adopt children?

Yes!

The new adoption tax credit
The Small Business Job Protection Act of 1996 contains a new tax credit for the costs associated with adoption. An extra bonus is that it also includes a provision for employers to pay adoption expenses as a tax-free employee fringe benefit.

Adoption tax credit
The 1996 tax act created a $5,000 tax credit for adoption expenses. This increases to $6,000 if the child is disabled or has special needs. There is no maximum credit per year or maximum number of children to which the credit may be applied.

New tax law will affect 1997 returns

The tax credit first becomes available for 1997 returns. It must be taken initially in the year after adoption expenses are first paid, and then again in the year the adoption becomes final. For example, take a situation in which you paid adoption expenses of $2,000 in 1997, $1,000 in 1998 and $3,000 in 1999. The first credit is available in tax year 1998 for the $2,000 paid in 1997. The balance of the $5,000 credit, or $3,000, is taken in 1999, when the adoption becomes final. For adoption of a child who is not a U.S. citizen or resident, the credit is the same, but may only be taken in the year of adoption, even if the expenses were paid in one or more prior years. For such an adoption, using the above example, there would be a $5,000 credit available only in 1999, the year the adoption became final.

Note: after 2001, only adoptions of children with special needs will qualify for the tax credit.

Adoption credit is limited by income
If your Adjusted Gross Income (AGI) is over $75,000, the credit starts to phase out proportionately until eliminated at an AGI of $115,000. The credit in any one year is limited to your tax liability. Any unused credit may be carried over for up to five years.

Which expenses qualify
The expenses that qualify for the credit are reasonable and necessary costs, including adoption fees, court costs, attorney fees, and other similar items that are related to the legal adoption of an eligible child. Note: expenses related to the adoption of your spouse's child do not qualify for the credit.

Eligible child
The new law defines an eligible child as either a person either under 18 years old, or an individual physically or mentally unable to care for himself or herself. The higher $6,000 credit for children with special needs is only available for the adoption of a U.S. citizen or resident. For foreign adoptions, the credit expires after the year 2001.

Employer adoption plans
Beginning in 1997, if your employer pays or reimburses you for the cost of adoption, you can exclude that amount up to $5,000 per child ($6,000 for special needs children) from your income, as long as the adoption expenses are paid under an adoption assistance program set up by your employer.

If your company does not have such a plan, it may simply be because it's new. Ask about it. For more information, the IRS has released Publication 968, "Tax Benefits for Adoption." To file for the credit, use the new Form 8839, "Qualified Adoption Expenses."

69 I will be turning 65 on January 1, 1998. Can I claim the extra standard deduction for 1997?

Yes. For some strange reason, the IRS considers you 65 on the day before your 65th birthday. So anyone who turns 65 on January 1 is treated for tax purposes as if they were 65 on December 31 of the prior year.

70 I paid my mother's funeral bill from her own money. Can this be deducted on her final income tax return?

No. Funeral and burial expenses are not deductible on personal tax returns even if paid from the decedent's own funds. However, the expenses are a deductible item on the decedent's estate tax return if there is a taxable estate.

71 What is the difference between an exemption and a deduction? They seem like the same thing to me.

An exemption is a special type of tax deduction you receive for your dependents, usually your spouse, your children, and yourself. The deduction for personal exemptions is a specific amount, as opposed to other deductions, which may be different, depending on how much you spend for the deductible item. In 1997, each personal exemption gives you a $2,650 tax deduction.

72 Can you suggest any good tax shelters in which to invest my money? I need deductions!

No. We don't do that anymore. That was the 80's, remember? Invest for profits, not for losses. If you need deductions that badly, give your accountant a raise—it's tax-deductible. You could also buy 1,000 copies of this book and give them out to your cabinet members and high level political advisors.

Section 5
Your Questions About Home Office Deductions

The propensity to truck, barter and exchange one thing for another…is common to all men, and to be found in no other race of animals.
   Adam Smith

It's the 90's, and more people are working from their homes than ever before. Even people who commute to primary jobs often have a small business which they run from their home. Unfortunately, tax law has lagged way behind the way people actually live and work. Frankly, many of the laws in this area just don't make sense anymore.

The good news is that relief is oh-so-slowly on the way. The new tax act will make it easier to qualify for the home office deduction…but you have to wait two more years. So, for your 1997 and 1998 taxes, the tough home office rules will still generally apply.

Here's the good news…for 1999, that is:

Home offices
Beginning in 1999, the tax law is amended to specifically provide that the home office now qualify as a principal place of business—even if the office is used by the taxpayer to conduct mainly or solely administrative or management activities of his or her trade or business—as long as there are no other fixed locations or offices where such business could have been conducted. The new law effectively reverses the landmark Supreme Court ruling that denied the home office deduction based on a narrow interpretation of the "principal place of business" rules. To qualify, even under the new rules, the office still must be used exclusively and regularly as a place of business by the taxpayer. And if the taxpayer is an employee, she or he only qualifies for a home office deduction if the office is used solely for the convenience of the employer.

New tax law will affect future returns

Good tax law

My aim in this section is to simplify the home office tax rules so that even a congressional aide—who probably wrote the rules—could understand them. Hopefully, you'll be able to spend less time in your accountant's office and more time running your business.

73. What exactly is the "home office deduction"?

There is, technically speaking, no such thing. The term is used by everyone—including CPAs—to describe the group of expenses relating to the business use of your home that may be deductible against your wages or business income.

If you qualify under the tough rules (see *Question #74*), you must first categorize the expenses into direct expenses and indirect expenses. The next step is to figure out how many (by percentage) of these expenses are business and how many are personal and thus nondeductible.

Direct expenses

The IRS describes direct expenses as those that "benefit only the business part of your home." These items are deductible in full. No allocation needs to be made for personal use, since direct expenses by definition apply 100% to business. Examples of direct expenses are: repairs or painting of only the area used as a home office or the cost of cleaning only the business portion of the home.

- *For the self-employed, direct expenses are reported on your federal tax return on Form 8829, "Expenses For Business Use of Your Home."*

- *If you're an employee using your home for business as a convenience to your employer, you deduct the expenses on Schedule A as a miscellaneous itemized deduction, subject to the 2% limit on Adjusted Gross Income (AGI).* If you do not itemize, you cannot claim the deductions.

Indirect expenses

Indirect expenses are those that apply to the entire home, of which only a portion are deductible as a home office business expense. The deductible portion is based on the square footage of the room or area used for business as compared to square footage of the entire home. For example, if the total area of the home is 2,000 square feet and the area used for business is 200 square feet, then 10% (200 divided by 2,000 square feet) of your indirect expenses is deductible. Therefore, in this example, if insurance on your home is $1,000, then 10%, or $100, qualifies as a business expense. Other indirect expenses include: mortgage interest, real estate taxes, rent, casualty losses, repairs, utilities, security systems, depreciation, and any other expense directed to the upkeep of the entire home.

The non-business portion of items that may be deductible elsewhere on the return, such as mortgage interest, real estate taxes, and casualty losses, are deducted as itemized deductions on Schedule A if you itemize. The deduction for indirect expenses that are not deductible as itemized deductions can be limited, depending on the income of your business, and cannot be used to create a loss. Deductions that exceed the allowable limit can be carried over to future years. Indirect expenses are claimed on Form 8829 if you're self-employed.

74. What requirements do I need to fulfill to entitle me to a home office deduction for tax year 1997?

1997 and 1998: IRS rules still tough for home office deductions

If you're thinking about taking a home office deduction in 1997 or 1998, you should be aware of the changes which took place as a result of a 1993 Supreme Court decision, which makes it tougher on people who do some, but not all, of their work at home.

U.S. Supreme Court ruling

On January 12, 1993, the high court decided that Dr. Nader Soliman, a self-employed anesthesiologist, was not entitled to the home office deduction he had claimed. Dr. Soliman worked in three hospitals, none of which provided him office space to do paperwork, maintain records, do research, or keep in phone contact with patients. Rather than rent an outside office, Dr. Soliman decided to set apart a spare bedroom in his apartment to use as his exclusive business office. The IRS challenged him several times, and lost each time, except for the last time, when it won a landmark decision defeating Dr. Soliman's—and many other people's—home office deduction. (This all changes, though, beginning in 1999.)

Principal place of business

The Supreme Court's 1993 ruling spelled out guidelines for claiming a home office deduction. As a general rule, a home office is only deductible if it is used exclusively and regularly as a principal place of business, or to meet with patients, clients, or customers in the normal course of business. If you're an employee, you must be able to show that the home office is maintained for the convenience of your employer. However, if your only business location is in your home, it is easier to qualify. Examples include: freelance writer, mail order business operator, or doctors, accountants, and lawyers. Others, like Dr. Soliman, who work both in the home and at outside locations, must for the present time, show which location is the more important one.

1997-'98 IRS rules—the "relative importance" test

IRS has revised its Publication 587, "Business Use of Your Home," to reflect the two new factors identified by the Supreme Court. These are:

- *The relative importance of the activities performed at each business location*

- *The time spent at each location*

The "relative importance" test will be applied first, to determine which location is the principal place of business. If a principal place of business cannot be determined, then the time test will be applied to see where you spend most of your time. These tests can result in a taxpayer having no principal place of business. The home office deduction will be allowed only if the home is considered to be the principal place of business under the 1997-'98 rules.

The relative importance test determines where the essential income earning activities take place. According to the IRS, the most important job is earning money, and the principal place of work will be the place where that money is earned. The place where income is earned is the place where you see customers, make sales, take orders, and perform services for which you're paid. All other functions are of less importance. These include administrative, bookkeeping, and management tasks performed at the home office, even if you hire someone to work full-time there. Although these functions may be essential from a business point of view, they are not considered the most important functions under the "relative importance" test.

In short, if you work full-time from your home, or do some, but not all your work out of an office in your home, you may (for the 1997 tax year) qualify for the home office deduction if your home is the principal place of business and is used exclusively and regularly in your business.

75 **I am a self-employed plumber. I use a room in my home exclusively as a home office to make customer calls, set up appointments, prepare job estimates, do paperwork, and keep my files. I also hire a full time office person who works in my home office answering calls, handling problems, and helping me schedule my day. Do I qualify for the home office deduction?**

No. And please, don't shoot the messenger! Although Congress fixed the problem beginning in 1999, you'll have to live with the old rules until then. So, for right now, you don't qualify, because your most essential function is plumbing, which is done at your customers' homes, not at your home office.

Here's what the IRS will allow, though: have your customers bring their sinks and toilets to your home so that you can fix them there. Now you qualify, since the essential function of your business, plumbing services, is being performed in your home. This will also reduce your taxes significantly, because you will no longer have any customers or income to tax!

76 **I am a college professor, and as a teacher I am required to do a considerable amount of work in a room in my home that is used regularly and exclusively for my school-related work. I grade papers there, prepare lesson plans, and do research for at least two to three hours a night. I actually put in more time at home than I do in the classroom. Am I entitled to the home office deduction?**

No.

Even teachers fail the tax tests
Based on its Supreme Court victory, the IRS has issued strict rules on who can qualify for the home office deduction. The ruling cites examples of how the IRS applies the home office tests. In each scenario, the assumption is that the home office is used exclusively and regularly for business. This gives you an idea of how tough the criteria are, since you can use a part of your home exclusively and regularly for business, and still not be allowed to claim a home office deduction.

Teachers lose

To remove all doubts, the IRS has specifically denied the home office deduction to teachers. They take the position that a teacher's income is earned in the classroom where the teacher is paid to teach, regardless of additional responsibilities outside the classroom. This ruling places great weight on where you "deliver" your services, which for teachers means that school is the principal place of business.

Some exceptions include: home tutoring of students who paid you privately, and writing which produced income separate from your teaching wages.

77 I rent my home. Can I take the home office deduction?

Hot tip!

Yes, as long as you qualify under the regular home office rules, which means that you can deduct only the portion of your rent that represents the actual space (square footage) that is used exclusively for business. As a matter of fact, it's the best way to take the deduction. If you are a homeowner, part of the home office deduction that you would take is depreciation of the business portion of your home. The problem of "depreciation recapture" when you sell the home is avoided because rent can never be recaptured since you cannot sell a property that you do not own. The rent for the home office portion of your home, on the other hand, is deductible with no further tax consequences. (For more on depreciation recapture see *Questions #110 and #155*.)

78 How on earth then, does one qualify for the elusive home office deduction?

If you work mainly outside the home and use the home solely as an office, it will be tough to get the deduction. If you regularly see customers or clients at your home office you may still qualify, even if your home is not your principal place of business.

What helps? Significant income-producing functions should be moved to the home office, if possible. New technology such as computers, fax machines, and modems make this easier for some businesses. Look for ways to segregate home office business expenses from personal residential expenses. Setting up your business space in a separate structure, not attached to the home, will also help your case. For example, an artist's studio, a florist's greenhouse, or a carpenter's workshop can be set up in an unattached garage or other freestanding structure. Arrange for separate utility hookups and separate insurance bills for the business space. Also, try to keep meticulous records of the amount of time spent at the home office versus other outside business locations.

If you're a self-employed doctor, accountant, dentist, attorney, or in any other type of business where essential job functions are performed in the home office, you will most likely qualify for the home office deduction. If you're a writer with a home office where you do your writing, you will probably qualify, even if you spend significant time away from your home office conducting interviews, taking photos, or doing research, because writing is your most essential function—the one that earns you your income—and it's done in your home office.

The home office deduction is claimed on IRS Form 8829, "Expenses for Business Use of Your Home." You should also obtain IRS Publication 587, "Business Use of Your Home," for detailed information and examples about how the IRS will rule in specific situations.

79 **What about all the office equipment I use in my home office, like file cabinets, a copier, desks, and office supplies? If I do not qualify for the home office deduction, does that mean that I cannot deduct these expenses either?**

Not at all. You can deduct these items.

Other expenses

Whether or not you qualify for the home office deduction, you can still deduct all business expenses that are not for the use of your home, or for expenses incurred in the home, such as wages paid to employees who work for you in your home office. Supplies, stationery, postage, dues, business telephone expenses, and depreciation of equipment used in the home office are also deductible. These are not classified as either direct or indirect home office expenses because they are not for the use of your home. They are separate expenses of running your business. They are deductible in full and not subject to the allocation rules for home office expenses.

Home office tax deduction for storage

Since 1996, one small break allows you to deduct expenses allocated to a separate portion of your home used to store inventory or product samples.

80 Is there any down side to taking the home office deduction?

Tax trap!

Yes. Welcome to a big, fat tax trap. If you're claiming a room or part of your house as business property or a home office, that part of the property no longer qualifies for the favorable tax treatment that a personal residence receives when the house is sold.

For example, your home office won't be eligible for the $125,000 capital gains exclusion (for those 55 and over) and it won't be eligible for the new tax law that exempts $500,000 ($250,000 for singles) of gain on the sale of your personal residence from tax. You basically nail your own coffin here, because you have to declare and prove to the IRS that you use part or all of your home for business in order to qualify for the home office deductions that you claim. But once you do, you have also told the IRS that the "business" part of your home is no longer a personal residence, and you therefore no longer qualify for the tax breaks available when you sell your personal residence. So it may not always be best to claim home office deductions or turn homes into business properties for tax reasons.

Another problem with the home office deduction comes when and if you decide to sell the home. While operating your home office, you will be taking yearly deductions on the depreciation of the business portion of your home. With depreciation you're writing off part of the cost of your home, which sounds pretty good until the day comes when you sell that home and have to give back those depreciation deductions. (For more on this issue see *Questions #110 and #155*.)

There is a way around this trap (isn't that why you bought this book?). The solution: don't call it a home office anymore. Take the "keep out" sign off the door, invite the children in to mess up the room (this can be done in less than five minutes, trust me!), and move a TV in there. Now you no longer have a room exclusively used for business. You have disqualified yourself from taking the home office deduction, but you now qualify for even bigger tax breaks. But you must discontinue your home office two years prior to the sale (for more on this, see *Question #147*).

81. Will taking the home office deduction trigger a tax audit?

Not necessarily, although many tax commentators and writers will tell you that it might. This was more arguably the case a few years ago when fewer people were working and running businesses from their homes. But times have changed, and there are so many people working at home that the IRS simply cannot audit everyone who claims a home office deduction. Of course, any deduction that exceeds certain limits may trigger an audit, whether or not the home office deduction is claimed. (See *Question #161* for more details on audit triggers and red flags.)

Never avoid taking a tax deduction because you fear a tax audit, unless you really do have something to hide. Report the information correctly, and according to the instructions on the tax forms. Not following the format or being sloppy about presenting the information might very well trigger an audit. This is an area where you may need a CPA or other professional tax preparer to make sure the tax information is correctly stated on your return, and to be certain that you receive the maximum benefit from your home office. A tax professional may also be better able to represent you if you do get audited.

Section 6
Your Questions About Your Business and Taxes

Being good in business is the most fascinating kind of art... Making money is art and working is art and good business is the best art.
   Andy Warhol

From the very first day that they open their doors, business owners need answers to tax questions that can literally make or break their efforts to become successful. Experience has taught me that business owners—who are accustomed to having to make decisions quickly—often act first and ask questions later. But whether you have been in business for months or years, or are just getting started on planning your new business, this section is for you.

I'll cover such key issues as personal liability, tax exposure, IRS reporting requirements, and, of course, what all business owners ask most: how to pay less tax. (That's where those business tax deductions come in handy.) So, read on!

82 I just started my own business. Should I be incorporated?

You should consult both your accountant and your attorney on this issue. Corporations are not for everyone, especially start-ups. Since most new businesses start slowly, it is often a good idea to begin simply, as a sole proprietorship, until you get your feet wet and really start to find your niche.

Hot tip!

Corporations are expensive to set up—you'll spend $500 to $750 in legal fees. Then there are annual filing fees, and state franchise and corporation taxes, not to mention the cost of hiring an accountant to prepare the corporation tax returns and numerous corporate filings throughout the year. If your business changes direction, which often happens to start-ups, you may want to change your name or start a new, better defined corporation. This will mean more accounting and legal costs consumed in closing down your old corporation and changing to a new name or new entity.

As a new business owner you must be able to devote your limited capital to operating your business. Keep the administrative, accounting, and legal costs to a minimum. After all, these costs do not produce income and you need income or you will be out of business before you even get started.

In short, starting out simple as a sole proprietorship is the easiest and least expensive form of business to operate.

83 How do I decide when to incorporate my business as it grows?

This decision depends on the type of business and the potential liability you may be exposed to through the products or services you profer. If you're a professional—a doctor, lawyer, CPA, architect, or engineer—a corporation will not shield you from your own liability or malpractice. You need separate malpractice insurance for that. If you're selling a product that lends itself to potential lawsuits, then a corporation will generally shield your personal assets from such claims. This applies, for example, if you're selling a toy or household item that is poorly manufactured and causes an injury or death. It also applies if you're selling a food item that later turns out to cause cancer (doesn't everything?).

84 If I incorporate, what type of corporation should I have?

There are two types: you can choose between a regular corporation (designated a "C corporation") or a small business corporation (designated an "S corporation"). Most small businesses are better off starting out as an S corporation, especially since the new legislation in the Small Business Job Protection Act of 1996, signed into law by President Clinton on August 20, 1996, expanded many of the tax advantages to S corporations.

85 What are my other choices besides a corporation?

You can be a sole proprietorship, a partnership (for two or more individuals in a business) or a relatively new entity, called a limited liability company, which is now available in nearly every state.

86. If I decide not to incorporate my business, how can I protect my personal assets from liability?

If you're not incorporated or organized as a limited liability company, your assets remain unprotected. The only thing you can and should do is carry higher business liability insurance. There are specialized types, depending on your trade or business. This is a small price to pay to protect yourself from the telephone-number jury awards being handed out these days.

87. How do I become an S corporation?

Contrary to popular belief, this is not automatic upon formation of your corporation. You must elect S corporation status by filing IRS Form 2553, (Election by a Small Business Corporation) within the first 75 days of the corporation's tax year. For a calendar year corporation (one whose tax year ends on December 31), the election must be filed by March 15 of the year. You should receive confirmation from the IRS within 30 days of filing your election. Unfortunately, many business owners are unaware that they must elect S corporation status, and do nothing, thinking that the lawyer who set up the corporation took care of it. This is a tax election and is usually done by your business accountant at the same time that he or she helps you apply for a Federal Employer Identification Number (EIN) on IRS Form SS-4. If you missed the initial filing, see the next question.

88. I started a new business and my attorney set up my corporation. I was advised to set up an S corporation, and I thought this was done by my attorney, but apparently not. Is there any way I can correct the problem retroactively?

Until 1997 you would have been out of luck, but now the answer is "yes."

Relief for late-filed "S" corporation elections
The IRS has provided relief for late S corporation elections. If you want to elect S status for your corporation, you must file Form 2553, "Election by a Small Business Corporation," within 2½ months after the beginning of your taxable year. For 1998 calendar year corporations, the election would has to be filed with IRS by March 15, 1998. Many new businesses miss this date because owners think the election is automatic, or

New tax law will affect 1997 returns

because they believed the attorney who formed the corporation took care of it.

The IRS has now provided a six-month extension for the election. A 1998 calendar year corporation that misses the March 15, 1998 due date now has until September 15, 1998 to elect S corporation status and file Form 2533 with the IRS.

The IRS will then determine if you have reasonable cause and notify you of their decision. Reasonable cause could simply be not knowing the tax rules or thinking that your S corporation status was taken care of by the attorney or other advisor who set up the corporation. There is no word yet about whether states which allow S corporations will also honor this extension. However, inn any case, this is long overdue relief.

89. We used to be an S corporation but switched to a C corporation designation. Now that Congress has made so many favorable changes for S corporations, I want to switch us back to an S corporation. Can I do this?

Yes. In the past, you had to wait five years and get IRS permission, but this is no longer necessary. However, the truth is that most S corporations do not switch to C corporations, and the ones that do will not find any advantage in switching back. For most small businesses, S corporations remain the best choice; unfortunately, the new S corporation tax laws have done little to help them. Has anyone ever explained what a small business is to Congress? Maybe, but they are still clueless.

90. As a new business owner, what income taxes should I be aware of?

Did you think that there was some magic way to be exempt from income taxes if you're in your own business? Thanks to your pals in Congress, you actually pay even more in taxes, after you add the self-employment tax (SE) to the regular income tax you pay on your business income.

No matter how you structure your business, if it's profitable, there will generally be income taxes to pay. Sole proprietors, shareholders in S corporations, and partners and members of limited liability companies (who elect to be treated as partners) do not pay tax at the business level. The profits in these entities flow through to the individual owners', partners' or members' personal tax returns, where they are subject to both the individual income tax and—except for shareholders in S corporations—the SE tax. Since the taxes are reflected on the personal returns of the business owners, they are the personal liabilities of the individual owners.

Likewise, losses by the above-mentioned entities flow through to individuals' returns. If you're a sole proprietorship, losses are reported on your personal return, Form 1040, Schedule C, "Profit or Loss From Business."

If, on the other hand, you're a C corporation, losses as well as income do not flow through to the individual shareholders' returns, but stay within the corporation. If the C corporation incurs a loss, it cannot be used personally, but can be either carried over to future corporation tax years in which there are profits, or carried back to prior profitable years. These are known as net operating losses (NOLs). In a C corporation they may be carried back three years or carried forward for up to 15 years after the year of the NOL. Under the new tax law, NOLs for the tax years beginning after August 5, 1997 can be carried back only two years, but can be carried forward 20 years. To carry back an NOL you must actually amend the corporate tax return by filing Form 1120-X.

91. Why are the taxes on my small business income so high?

Because you're actually paying two taxes. This is an issue that virtually no politician can understand. For example, when they tell you that you're only paying a 28% tax rate on $40,000 of business income, they neglect (or just have no clue) that you must also pay—if your business is organized as sole proprietor, a partnership, or limited liability corporation (LLC)—an additional 15.3% self-employment (SE) tax, for a combined rate of 43.3%. And that is before you add on any state, and in some cases, city or other local taxes. That's right. You can actually be paying over 50% in tax at a modest income level, and it does not matter how many kids or other exemptions you might have. In fact, you may have taxable income (income after deductions) of zero, but you will still have a self-employment tax on your net business income. This is because the SE tax, unlike the income tax, cannot be reduced by any itemized deductions, personal exemptions for dependents, net operating losses, or other non-business deductions.

Really stupid tax law

Remember: the SE tax is a separate tax, in addition to the regular income tax. It is based solely on the net SE income from your trade or business, and the combined tax rate is 15.3%. The SE tax is made up of two taxes, Social Security (FICA) and Medicare. FICA is 12.4% of an annually increasing base amount ($65,400 for 1997) of net SE income. The Medicare tax is 2.9% and applies to all net SE income without any cap.

92 How is the self-employment tax paid?

Most people pay the tax by making quarterly estimated tax payments. An exception is if you have other wages from which tax is withheld for you by your employer. Keep in mind that the quarterly estimated tax payments should cover not just your SE tax, but all taxes owed, including income and capital gains tax. Remember, you may deduct one-half of the self-employment tax, and you don't have to itemize to get the deduction.

93 What deductions should I be taking to reduce taxes on my business?

Deductions are the key to paying less in taxes. The IRS considers just about anything deemed an ordinary or necessary expense of running your particular business as an allowable deduction. There are some basic tax deductions that practically every business should take advantage of. Here are some of the most common:

- *Contributions to your or your company's retirement plan* This can be one of the biggest tax breaks around.

- *Auto and truck expenses* If you use your car for business, you should be deducting the cost of the vehicle as well as the costs to maintain and run it, like: gas, oil, repairs, auto insurance, tires, license, and registration fees. You could also choose to take a standard mileage allowance, which for 1997 is 31.5 cents per business mile. Your deductions are limited to your business use. Commuting costs are not deductible.

- *Business meals and entertainment (limited to 50%)*

- *Business travel* This can cover trade shows, conventions, or seminars you attend locally or out of town.

- *Telephone* This includes your cellular phone, if you use it for business.

- *Business equipment* This includes all types of office equipment, including: copiers, computers, fax machines, furniture, and telephone systems. The cost of these equipment items are generally not entirely deductible in the year of purchase but must be depreciated ("written off") over a period of years (usually three, five, or seven years, depending on the type of equipment). You can also take advantage of first-year expensing (IRS Section 179, depreciation) and write off up to $18,000 (for 1997) in the first year. This will go higher in future years (see *Question #104* for more on first-year expensing).

- *Fees paid to contractors, lawyers, accountants, and other consultants, including commissions paid (remember to issue 1099 forms here)*

- *Insurance; advertising; repairs; rent; business interest; business, corporate, and payroll taxes; and utilities*

- *Professional, trade or union dues, licenses, subscriptions, and trade organization fees*

- *Office supplies, including just about anything you buy for your business at office superstores or your local stationer*

- *All payroll and related payroll tax costs*

This list goes on and on, and every deduction is worth money to you in tax savings. The general rule is to deduct anything that relates to running your business or which helps you get new business.

94 I'm self-employed. How much can I deduct for health insurance?

The new tax law will make health insurance fully deductible for the self-employed, beginning in 1997 with a deduction of 40%. It gradually steps up to 100% in 2007, as follows:

1998 through 1999 .... 45%
2000 through 2001 .... 50%
2002 .... 60%
2003 through 2005 .... 80%
2006 .... 90%
2007 .... 100%

New tax law will affect 1997 returns

New tax law will affect future returns

95. What is depreciation?

Depreciation is the method by which the government allows you to deduct (write off) the cost of an asset that is used for your trade or business. Depreciation deductions are limited, and must be taken over years (exception: first-year expensing—see *Question #104*).

The idea behind depreciation is that after a period of years these types of assets will need to be replaced, at which time their value is nil. The IRS allows you to deduct their decrease in value—or "depreciation"—over time.

96. How should I keep track of business deductions?

The best way is to keep a separate checking account solely for your business—you should not be commingling business and personal income and expenses. If you pay for most items with a business check, a year-end analysis of your business account will provide your accountant or tax preparer with a good list. Whatever you do not pay for by check, pay for with a credit card, if possible, then pay the credit card bills with a business check.

If paying cash for business items, retain a receipt, then use the receipts to reimburse yourself from the business checking account. Reimburse yourself monthly or quarterly, but don't let it go much longer than that. Remember: receipts become invaluable at tax audits. Even if you're not a good record-keeper, set up a box or large folder for the year. Mark it "1998," for example, and get into the habit of throwing every receipt in there. You can always have someone else go through it at the end of the year to sort it all out—but don't make that person your accountant, because it will cost you.

97. I just started my business and I have huge deductions but no income. Can I take the deductions on the first year's return even though I have no income?

Yes, but not for the full amount. These are referred to as start-up costs and generally must be amortized—deducted over time—over no less than 60 months. These expenses must be directly related to the opening of the business.

98. I tried to start a business but it failed. In the process, however, I incurred expenses. Can I deduct my losses?

That depends. Expenses incurred while you're still trying to decide what business to go into are personal and nondeductible. Such expenses include trips to evaluate potential investments or businesses.

However, if you have already decided on a specific business and invested in that business, but were unsuccessful in your attempt to get the business off the ground, you can deduct the expenses incurred as a capital loss. This includes items such as accounting and legal costs of setting up your corporation, rent paid, wages, advertising, telephone, utilities, etc. Capital losses of up to $3,000 per year are deductible against your other income (from wages, interest, dividends, pensions, etc.). Anything over $3,000 in losses can be carried over to future years or used to offset capital gains. There is no limit on the amount of capital losses that can be used to offset capital gains in a single year.

If, in addition to the expenses of setting up your business, you purchased office equipment, machines, trucks, computers, or other similar "fixed" assets, you cannot include the cost of these items in figuring your loss. Any deductible loss on these assets will be determined at the time you sell or dispose of them.

99. Should I buy or lease the auto that I use for business?

Lease. If you buy, you must depreciate the vehicle over a minimum of five years, usually longer, because yearly depreciation deductions on autos used for business have annual caps.

Hot tip!

The more expensive the car, the better the leasing deal becomes, because leasing deductions are not capped and they may therefore be written off faster. (There is a small "income add-back" which reduces the amount of the leasing deduction, but in general this is not enough to offset the advantages of leasing.) Leasing deductions, like depreciation deductions if you buy, are limited by the proportion of business use. For example, if you use your car only 80% for business, then 80% of the lease payments is a business expense, and the remainder must be paid out of your personal funds.

Here are the annual depreciation caps for your purchased business car:

First year of ownership *$3160*
Second year of ownership *$5000*
Third year of ownership *$3050*
Fourth and all subsequent years of ownership *$1775*

100 Do I need an accountant for my small business?

Yes. Being a CPA myself, isn't there only one possible answer here? But seriously, the biggest and most common mistakes occur when businesses are started with poor advice or none. Even from the very beginning, an accountant can advise you on how to structure your business, what kind of taxes to expect, how to raise capital, how to set up your books, and how to keep your hard-earned profits from being downsized by taxes. You also do not want to worry about making mistakes, which can cost you in lost tax deductions, missed filing dates, or IRS penalties for not knowing the tax rules. Of course, you can fill out forms, prepare payroll, and keep your books yourself, but do you want to? Your time is probably better spent running your business.

How much of an accountant's time you'll need depends on the size and nature of your business. If you're starting out small, as most businesses do, you may only need to see your accountant on an annual or quarterly basis. As your business grows, though, you may find that you need to hire a bookkeeper so that your books and records don't fall behind, in which case you'll be paying an accountant to fix up the mess and bring you up to date. Once your business starts to take off and you're writing hundreds of checks a year and increasing profitability, you might be ready to have your accountant work for you on a monthly basis, recording your checks and deposits, checking bank balances, and providing you with financial statements and tax advice.

101 I am hiring an employee. What taxes should I be aware of?

You don't want to know. But since you asked, I'll tell you. This is a complicated issue, which is why payroll services are so profitable.

As soon as you hire an employee, you must have them fill out a W-4 form ("Employee's Withholding Allowance Certificate") which lists his or her name, address, Social Security number, marital status, and the number of personal exemptions he or she claims. You do not need to send it to the IRS, unless more than ten exemptions are claimed, but you must keep it on file. New employees must also complete Form I-9 ("Employment Eligibility Verification") for the Immigration and Naturalization Service (INS). Yes, as an employer you're also a secret agent for the INS. How exciting! Form I-9 must also remain on file at your place of business for possible INS inspections and the penalties for not having the INS forms are steep. All employees should also have Social Security numbers.

With your first employee you become responsible for filing a flock of forms and paying a plethora of payroll taxes, including the following:

- *Withholding taxes* These are taxes withheld from your employees' wages which you're required to turn over to the IRS and to your state tax department. These include: Social Security (FICA), Medicare tax, and federal and state income taxes. The FICA and Medicare taxes are based on a percentage of the employees' wages. The FICA is 6.2% of the first $65,400 (the 1997 limit) of wages, and the Medicare tax is 1.45% of all wages. The federal and state withholding taxes vary depending on each employee's marital status and the number of personal exemptions they claim when they fill out their W-4 form.

- *Employer matching* The employer must match the withheld FICA and Medicare taxes and pay them to the IRS along with the employees' share. The employees' FICA and Medicare taxes, and the employer's matching shares, along with any federal income tax withheld from employees' wages, are paid to the IRS by making Federal Tax Deposits (FTD) to your bank with Form 8109 ("Federal Tax Deposit Coupon"). You must have a Federal Tax Deposit Coupon Booklet containing the coupons. If you do not, write to your local IRS office to request one. Employees' wages, along with FICA, Medicare, and federal withholding tax liability, as well as a record of your tax deposits, are reported quarterly to the IRS on Form 941. Form 941 is due within one month after the close of the calendar quarter. New regulations concerning mandatory electronic filing of payroll taxes for some businesses were scheduled to go into effect on July 1, 1997, but were delayed.

- *Federal Unemployment Tax (FUTA)* Most wages are subject to this tax as well as state unemployment tax (SUTA). In *most* states this tax is paid entirely by the employer and is not withheld from employees' wages. FUTA is based on the first $7,000 of annual wages for each employee (other than certain family members, spouse, and minor children). The tax rate is 6.2%, but most employers receive a federal credit of up to 5.4% for state unemployment tax paid. Therefore, the net rate is usually only 0.8% of the first $7,000 of annual wages per employee, for a maximum of $56 ($7,000 multiplied by 0.8% equals $56) per employee per year (less if the employee earns less than $7,000 in a calendar year). If you do not pay, or if you are exempt from state unemployment taxes, then you must pay the full 6.2% FUTA rate.

FUTA is paid either quarterly, using the Federal Tax Deposit (FTD) coupons (if the liability exceeds $100), or with IRS Form 940 (or short Form 940-EZ) which is filed annually by January 31, after the calendar year-end.

102 Can I put my kids on the payroll and deduct the wages I pay them?

Yes. But they must actually work and the pay must be reasonable. In other words, you cannot pay your six year-old VP $150,000 a year. There are other breaks, too. If you are an unincorporated business—a "sole proprietorship"—and your child is less than 18, the child is not subject to FICA (Social Security and Medicare tax) or unemployment taxes.

The child can further offset his or her wages by contributing up to $2,000 per year to an IRA.

Now, if you could only get them to actually work!

103 What must I do if I pay an independent contractor?

Tax trap!

The first thing is to make sure that the person you're paying is truly an independent contractor by IRS standards. There are numerous rules and regulations in this area which you should check on with your accountant, but the bottom line is that if the person you pay receives most or all of their income from you, and works under your control with tools or equipment you provide, that person is probably not an independent contractor.

The IRS will feel free to reclassify such a person as your employee. You would then be responsible for all the payroll taxes and employee benefits mentioned in *Question #101*, directly above. This could be a costly affair, so be careful here.

Any independent contractor that you pay $600 or more must be issued a 1099 Form. The 1099 reports the name, address, and Social Security number or EIN of the recipient, as well as the amount paid over the calendar year. They must be given to the recipient independent contractor by January 31 of the year following the year in which the money was earned. There is a $50 penalty (up to $100,000 a year) for each 1099 or W-2 you fail to provide to recipients. This penalty also applies if information on the form is incorrect. The IRS also requires a copy of all your 1099s.

104 I run my own business and purchased a computer system that cost $12,000. How much of this cost can I deduct this year?

Possibly the entire $12,000. Under Internal Revenue Code Section 179, you're entitled, in 1997, to deduct up to $18,000 (this amount rises to $18,500 in 1998 and increases in annual increments to $25,000 in 2003), of equipment other than autos (but including heavy trucks or vans) used in your business. The deduction is limited to your net income, but any amount not used can be carried over to future years. Make sure to claim the deduction for first-year expensing, even if your income limits you to no deduction. If you do not claim it (on Form 4562) in the first year, you do not get the carryover to future years when you may be able to claim it. The $18,000 (for 1997) starts to phase out on a dollar-for-dollar basis when you have purchased more than $200,000 worth of equipment during the tax year. When equipment purchases total $218,000, the first-year expensing election is disallowed. To use first-year expensing, you must elect it by filing Form 4562 and attaching it to your income tax return. The election must be made on your original return or on an amended return, filed before the due date of the original return including extensions.

Good tax law

Limitations in equipment deductions

The Section 179 (first-year expensing) deduction may be applied to your income from the business, to any other active trade or business, or to your wages as an employee of your own business.

For example, if you purchased a $12,000 computer for your business, and your business shows an income of $5,000 (before the deduction for the computer), you can deduct $5,000 because your deduction is limited by your business income of $5,000. You can then carry over the remaining $7,000 of unused Section 179 deduction to a future tax year.

Now let's add to this example the fact that you have wages as an employee of $20,000 for the year. Your W-2 wages count as active trade or business income, and are added to the $5,000 of business income, giving you an income limit of $25,000 ($5,000 plus the W-2 income of $20,000 equals $25,000). You may now deduct the entire $12,000 you paid for the computer in one year. Wages may be from any source, for example, from your own business or an outside employer.

Business tax break gets even better...first-year expensing increased

Business equipment may be new or used and mainly includes fixed assets such as: machinery, copiers, fax machines, computers, printers, telephone systems, office equipment, file cabinets, and other similar property used more than 50% in your active trade or business. It does not apply to real estate (home and buildings used for business) and is limited for most autos.

New increased deduction

The 1997 limit, which is the maximum amount that you can deduct in the first year, is $18,000. The first-year expensing deduction will increase as follows:

New tax law will affect future returns

Year	Amount
1997	$18,000
1998	$18,500
1999	$19,000
2000	$20,000
2001	$24,000
2002	$24,000
2003	$25,000

105 **In the example above, could I still get the full $12,000 deduction if I had no other wages or business income, but my spouse had the W-2 wages of $20,000 and we file a joint return?**

Yes!!! Your spouse's wages count for this rule. What a country!

Good tax law

106 **My husband and I have our own, separate businesses. Can we each take the maximum $18,000 deduction for 1997 first-year expensing? Can we actually deduct up to $36,000 because we have separate businesses?**

You must be dreaming. First-year expensing is good, but the IRS would never let it get that good. You are limited on your joint return to the maximum first-year expensing limit, which is $18,000 for 1997.

107 **Regarding that last question, what if my spouse and I file separately? Now can we each claim our $18,000 first-year expensing deduction?**

Wake up! You're still dreaming. Do you actually think they haven't thought of that? If you file married separately, that $18,000 limit becomes half, or $9,000 each, or any other way you want to split it up; but together, adding up the two returns, you cannot exceed $18,000. But good try! This is one of those areas where the marriage penalty gets you because, as two single individuals, you could each claim up to $18,000—or a total of $36,000.

108 **Must I use the Section 179 (first-year expensing) deduction if I do not need the deductions in the year of purchase?**

No. It is purely an election. But you can only elect it in the year of purchase. That is why they call it "first-year" expensing. It may pay to claim it, though, if only to have the full amount available in future years as a carryover. Or you can use the regular depreciation percentages and depreciate the $12,000 cost over five years.

On the other hand, if you need deductions because your non-business income places you in a high tax bracket, you can use the regular depreciation methods (five years in this case) to gain a deduction when first-year expensing nets you a zero deduction due to the business income limitations. Regular depreciation methods are not subject to the income limitations of Section 179, so you still get a deduction when you need it, but it will take more years to accrue the full benefit than if the Section 179 deduction had been used.

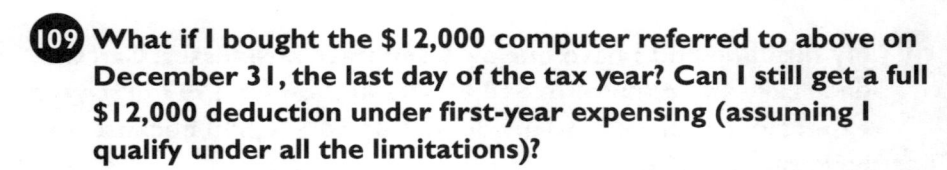

109 What if I bought the $12,000 computer referred to above on December 31, the last day of the tax year? Can I still get a full $12,000 deduction under first-year expensing (assuming I qualify under all the limitations)?

Yes. That's called tax leverage. But it gets even better!

No money down!

For super maximum tax leverage, you can get the full deduction without taking one cent out of your pocket when you buy. If you purchase it on a credit card or finance it with a business loan, without any money down, you still receive a full $12,000 deduction in the year you purchased it, and you can even deduct the interest as a business expense as you pay it.

This is starting to sound like an infomercial for first-year expensing!

110 I sold property that I used in my business. How do I calculate gain or loss on the sale and figure the tax?

Selling business property is likely to trigger what is referred to as "depreciation recapture." This means paying tax at ordinary income tax rates as opposed to capital gains rates on the depreciation you have deducted in previous years. As a result, any gain made on the sale of a property up to the full amount of the depreciation taken in past years is taxed at personal rates, at a maximum of 39.6%, compared with the maximum of 20% for capital gains. The rationale for this complexity is that when you deducted depreciation, you received a deduction against ordinary income and the IRS naturally wants you to pay it back that way. Get yourself a tax pro for figuring this stuff out.

There are two types of property that, when sold, may involve depreciation recapture. The IRS refers to these two types by code section. The first type is known as 1245 property (machinery and equipment) and the second type is 1250 property (real estate).

1245 property: equipment

This category includes depreciable property such as: equipment, machinery, office equipment, furniture, fixtures, autos, trucks, vans, computers, copiers, and any other personal property. When you sell 1245 property at a gain—and for the IRS a "gain" can occur even when you sell at a loss—the IRS insists that it recapture your depreciation deductions taken in prior years.

Example:

You buy a machine, used in your business, in 1993 for $10,000. You sell it in 1997 for $5,000. You have taken yearly depreciation deductions totaling $6,800.

First step: *What is your gain?*

The gain is $1,800. Here's how it's calculated: Your adjusted basis for tax purposes is $3,200 (the $10,000 original cost less the $6,800 in depreciation taken equals $3,200). The selling price of $5,000 less the adjusted basis of $3,200 equals the gain of $1,800.

Second step: *How much of your gain is recaptured (taxed at ordinary income tax rates as opposed to capital gains)?*

The total gain of $1,800 is taxed at ordinary income tax rates, not at capital gains rates. Any gain up to the full $6,800 taken in depreciation would be taxable at personal rates, while any gain above $6,800 would be taxable at the lower capital gains rates.

Now let's change this example so that the sale price is $12,000. What is the gain and how much of it will be taxed at ordinary income tax rates? Again, your adjusted basis for tax purposes is $3,200. Since the selling price is now $12,000, the total gain becomes $8,800. Of the $8,800 gain, the amount of depreciation previously taken—$6,800—is taxed at personal rates, while the balance of the gain—$2,000—is taxed at capital gains rates.

1250 property: real estate

This category includes depreciable real property such as two-family homes, apartment buildings, condos, buildings, structures, and residential and nonresidential real property. There is no depreciation recapture on 1250 property that you placed in service after 1986, but there are complicated recapture rules for real estate that is sold at a gain and was depreciated before 1986. Check with your accountant for details (see *Question #155* for details about the 25% tax rate on recapture under the new tax law).

111 **I have a full-time job where I participate in my employer's 401(k) plan. I have also started a business and would like to set up my own company plan. Am I entitled to contribute the maximum amount to my own company's plan (I own 100% of the company) if I am also contributing the maximum amount to my 401(k) at my full-time employer?**

Good tax law

Yes. Limits only apply when you have two or more companies which you control. "Control" for this purpose means that you either own the entire interest in the business or, for partnerships, that you own more than 50%. This is to prevent people from setting up multiple entities under their control, merely to avoid the pension contribution limits.

Remember, though, that individuals have an annual limitation of $9,500 in total contributions for all 401(k) plans. This will go up to $10,000 in 1998.

Section 7
Your Questions About Your Marriage and Taxes

Love at first sight is easy to understand; it's when two people have been looking at each other for a lifetime that it becomes a miracle.
   Sam Levenson

Tying the knot is a big deal, both for your personal life and your tax life. Nowadays both partners in most couples work, and when two working people marry, they are likely to discover the IRS's "marriage penalty." What I'm referring to is that no matter how you file as a married couple, you will pay more in taxes than if you continued filing as two single individuals. And generally, the higher your combined income, the greater the marriage penalty you will end up paying. Everyone's tax situation comes down to their own unique facts and circumstances, so you will want to have your tax pro run the numbers for you to see exactly how things will work out—financially, that is—before you say "I do." I'll give you the basics—and a bit more.

112 We are planning a December wedding, but a friend warned me to delay the wedding at least until the beginning of next year because of the "Marriage Tax." My fiancée and I both work and we each earn about the same annual salary. Should we be worried about a tax penalty for getting married this year?

The simple fact is that Uncle Sam would be happy to see you tie the knot as soon as possible—and not because he wants to see you living happily ever after. As an accountant, I have often advised my clients that delaying the nuptials until the following year might save them enough in taxes to pay for part of the celebration.

Here are some of the issues you need to consider to see if you will save taxes by remaining single a few more weeks…or even a few more years:

Two active wage earners? Watch out for the marriage penalty!
Partners who have similar incomes will be hit hardest, because they will end up in a tax bracket that reflects their combined income, as opposed to a bracket that is based on about one-half of their joint income. This is because our tax system works on graduated tax rates; as your taxable income increases, your tax rate also goes up. The federal income tax rates

Bad tax law

currently range from 15% to 39.6%. To give an example of how this affects the amount of tax you will pay, a two-earner couple with a joint Adjusted Gross Income (AGI) income of $44,000 would hit the 28% tax bracket on the last part of their income, while two single individuals who earned $22,000 each would never leave the 15% bracket. Although the actual marriage penalty in the above example is relatively low, about $200, it grows to thousands as combined income increases.

For example, when a couple's 1997 income exceeds $135,525 each, their joint income of $271,050 hits the top tax bracket of 39.6%. Two single individuals, however, could earn $271,050 *each* before reaching the 39.6% bracket. The difference is thousands of dollars in after-tax income.

If you think filing married separate solves the problem of the marriage penalty, think again (see *Question #116* for more on this).

Personal exemptions and the marriage penalty

For certain higher income taxpayers, personal exemptions, which for 1997 are $2650 for each exemption claimed, are phased out when AGI exceeds certain threshold amounts.

For those filing as individuals, as AGI exceeds the threshold amount of $121,200, personal exemptions begin to phase out, with full phaseout at $243,700. For married folks filing jointly, phaseout begins at $181,800 with full phaseout at $304,300. The two single individuals benefit by being able to earn $242,400 ($121,200 multiplied by 2) before their personal exemptions begin to be lost, whereas the married couple's exemptions begins phasing out when AGI hits $181,800. Two singles can therefore earn $60,600 more ($242,400 less $181,800) than if they were married, before they begin to lose their personal exemptions. As you may have guessed, the difference is even more dramatic when you add dependent children into the equation.

More bad news for married couples: IRA deductibility

If one spouse is an active participant in a company pension plan, both spouses' IRAs start to become nondeductible when the couple's combined AGI exceeds $40,000. The couple's IRA deductions are fully phased out when AGI hits $50,000 (beginning in 1998 these limits will increase—see *Question #182* for details). In contrast, the phaseout range for single individuals is from $25,000 to $35,000. Two singles can therefore earn

$50,000 before IRA deductions begin to phase out. One effect of this is that if only one spouse is a participant in the company pension, the non-pensioned spouse is automatically tainted, causing a nondeductible IRA. However, beginning in 1998 this will no longer be a problem (see *Question #182*). If the spouse who is not an active participant in a company pension were not married, he or she would not be subject to any phaseout of the IRA deduction. If neither spouse is an active participant in a company plan, then both spouses can contribute up to $2,000 to their own IRAs, and deduct this from their taxable income.

Medical expenses: still another marriage penalty

Here is another area where two-earner married couples usually pay more, by receiving less of a deduction. Medical expenses must reach 7.5% of AGI before they can be deducted, whether you're married or single. This means that single individuals will be in a position to have more deductible medical expenses than a married couple as long as most of the medical care was needed by one of them, which is usually the case when medical expenses are large. If, for example, your AGI is $100,000, you can only begin to deduct medical expenses when they exceed $7,500. Now let's say that each person in a couple had $50,000 of AGI and one of them had $6,000 in medical expenses, while the other had $1,000. If the spouse with the $6,000 of expenses had been able to file singly, he or she would have been able to deduct $2,250, figured by deducting the AGI limitation of $3,750 ($50,000 multiplied by 7.5%) from the $6,000. The other member of the couple would have had no deduction, since the $1,000 of medical expenses does not exceed the limitation. But once the two incomes are added together on a joint return, there is no medical deduction at all, since the $7,000 of total medical expenses does not exceed 7.5% of the combined income of $100,000.

Filing separately would allow a couple to have the same deductions as the two singles in the example above. Such a situation represents one of the few where it may pay for a married couple to file separately as opposed to jointly.

Other deductions: still another IRS blow to connubial bliss

Casualty, theft losses, and miscellaneous itemized deductions work in a similar fashion to medical expenses in that they, too, are subject to AGI percentage minimums before they can be deducted. Casualty and theft losses must exceed 10% of AGI (plus $100 for each loss) to be deductible.

Miscellaneous itemized deductions—which include work-related expenses, tax preparation fees, and investment expenses—must add up to 2% of AGI before they can be deducted. Itemized deductions are further subject to a reduction by 3% of the amount by which AGI exceeds $121,200 for 1997. (Medical and investment expenses, and casualty, theft, and gambling losses are exempt from this.) Since the same overall limitation applies to single individuals and married couples filing joint returns, two individuals who remain single can have an AGI double that of a married couple before the 3% disallowance of deductions kicks in.

The standard deduction: the final marriage penalty

If you do not have enough deductions to itemize, the tax law allows you to take a standard deduction. For 1997, single individuals are entitled to a standard deduction of $4,150; for married couples filing jointly the amount is $6,900. Here again, it quickly becomes apparent that two single individuals will receive a total standard deduction of $8,300 ($4,150 multiplied by 2), which exceeds the married jointly amount of $6,900 by $1,400. The favorable joint return tax rates may lessen the effect at lower income tax brackets, and in some cases, produce a lower overall tax for those who do not itemize. Again, as in the above section, it depends on who earned the income.

Senior citizens get hit too...

Senior citizens have equal opportunity when it comes to the marriage penalty (see *Question #203* for details).

113 Following up on the previous question, are there any potential tax advantages to our planned wedding?

For a few, a marriage "bonus"

The final strange twist to this saga of the tax implications of marriage is that when one spouse earns most or all of the income, there is no marriage penalty. In fact, it actually turns out to be a marriage "bonus," since the tax paid will be less than the combined tax of the two single individuals. This is because the joint tax rates when one spouse earns all or most of the income are less than the rates for a single individual with about the same income. The married couple filing jointly also can take advantage of a higher standard deduction, and they have two personal exemptions worth $2,650 each (in 1997) as compared to a single earner who has only one.

There are also situations where married couples filing jointly can have offsetting gains and losses, for example, if one partner sustains a large loss in the stock market or in a business in the same year in which the other has a gain.

114 Does the new tax legislation make it any better tax-wise to be married?

As my children say to me when I ask this type of question, "Uh duh… Hello?"

The new tax law creates so many marriage penalties that it is now beyond belief. Try these on for size:

New tax law will affect future returns

- *Student loan interest deductions (see **Question #42**)* By the year 2001, when fully phased in, two single people may each deduct up to $2,500 of student loan interest for a total of $5,000. If they were married the deduction would be limited to half of that amount, or $2,500. Also, the income limits for deducting student loan interest create a marriage penalty. Two single people can each have up to $40,000 of income or a total of $80,000 before the deduction begins to phase out. If they marry, their deduction would begin to phase out as their joint income exceeded $60,000, a $20,000 difference.

- *Education IRAs (see **Questions #42 and #46**)* The availability of the $500 per-child education IRA is phased-out for single people as each of their incomes exceed $95,000 or a total of $190,000. If they marry, the phaseout occurs at $150,000.

- *New Roth IRAs (see **Questions #169–#174**)* To qualify, two single people can each have up to $95,000 of income or a total of $190,000. If they marry, the income limit to qualify for a Roth IRA is $150,000.

- *Converting to the Roth IRA (see **Question #170**)* To qualify for the conversion, your income cannot exceed $100,000, whether single or married. This means that two single people, each with $100,000 or less of income—or up to a total of $200,000—can convert. If they marry, the limit is reduced to $100,000.

- *New IRA deductibility limits (see **Question #182**)* Under the new tax law, if you have a company pension plan, your IRA deduction may be limited. In the year 2005 for singles, and 2007 for married couples, two single people will still be able to make fully deductible IRA contributions with income of up to $50,000 each, or a total of $100,000 combined. If they marry, the limit is $80,000.

- *Child tax credits (see Question #66)* In 1998, for single people, the $400 child tax credit is phased out as each of their incomes exceed $75,000, or a total of $150,000. If they marry, the limit is $110,000.

Remember: the marriage penalty generally occurs only when both spouses work, and gets worse as both spouses' income increases. But all of the above new tax law items can be turned into a tax advantage—a marriage bonus—when one spouse earns most or all of the income. I had to end this answer with something positive about marriage. Write me if you can come up with any other advantages.

115 Can we keep our filing status as "single" after we are married and continue to pay at our own individual rates as we had before we were married?

No. Once you're married things change, and that goes for your filing status, too. Unfortunately, your filing status is not an option. Your status is determined as of the last day of the year. You must file as married if you were legally married as of December 31. The reverse is also true: if you happen to be an unmarried couple who would reap a tax benefit from a joint return, forget about it—joint returns are only available to those who tie the knot.

116 What's the difference between filing as married jointly and married separate?

If you're married, you generally have only two filing status options, married filing *jointly* or *separately*.

Married filing jointly means that you and your spouse file one tax return and you figure your tax using married jointly tax rates. Depending on which spouse earns the income, the married jointly tax rates are usually higher than if the same two people each filed as single individuals. This is the basis of the "marriage penalty" discussed above.

The difference between filing as married jointly and married separate is that filing separately requires each spouse to prepare their own return. When filing separately, each spouse figures their tax based on the tax rates for married filing separately. These rates contain no bargains. They are exactly one-half of the married filing jointly tax rates. All deduction and exemption limits are also split, and if one spouse itemizes, the other spouse filing separately must also itemize, even if he or she did not have enough deductions to itemize and would have fared better with the standard deduction.

Filing separately is designed so that you're not able to expand deductions or exemptions by splitting them up on separate returns. For example, the standard deduction for married jointly is $6,900 for 1997. For those filing married separate the standard deduction is exactly half of that amount, $3,450. For 1997, personal exemptions begin to phase out when Adjusted Gross Income (AGI) exceeds $181,800 (see *Question #67*) for married jointly returns. For married separate, the exemption phaseout begins at exactly half of that amount, $90,900. You rarely benefit from filing married separate.

In certain cases you may file as a "head of household," if you lived apart from your spouse for at least the last six months of the year, and you maintained the household for more than half the year for your child, who you can then claim as a dependent on your return. You file a separate return, but you may use the head of household rates, which are more favorable than either the married separate or the single rates. This usually applies when there are marital problems and one spouse leaves or abandons the other, or when a divorce is still not finalized on the last day of the year, but the spouses have been living apart. Head of household income brackets start out the same as single income brackets, but become lower as taxable income exceeds $24,650.

A general guideline: if one spouse earns all the income, then filing married jointly will generally produce a lower tax than if the two individuals were single and filed separate returns. However, spouses with roughly the same income would be subject to the marriage penalty, which becomes more severe as combined income increases.

117 **We have already filed married jointly, but we would have been better off filing married separately. Can we amend our return to change our filing status to married separately?**

No. Once you file jointly, you cannot go back and change it, unless you amend the return before April 15, the original due date of the return.

Check your facts carefully before changing from married filing jointly to married filing separately. There are very few situations where couples benefit from filing married separately. (See *Question #112* for details.)

118 **We are getting killed by the "marriage penalty" because we both work. We would save a bundle if we each filed as single individuals. Can we divorce for tax reasons in December, remarry in January, and then each file with the IRS as single?**

No. Although your filing status (married or single) is determined as of the last day of the tax year (December 31), it is a violation of tax law to divorce and remarry for the sole purpose of filing tax returns as unmarried individuals.

119 **Why do the tax laws make it so difficult for working married couples?**

Although, in the short run, it may seem that way, don't be discouraged. In the long run, our tax and legal system is actually more user-friendly to married couples who enjoy the long-term legal protection and gift and estate tax advantages generally denied to unmarried couples. I'll be talking more about these advantages in the Section 14, *Your Estate Planning and Taxes*.

Section 8
Your Questions About Living Together Unmarried

Marriage is a great institution, but I'm not ready for an institution.
  Mae West

There are approximately 4.2 million American households with unmarried partners, according to the United States Census Bureau's 1990 survey. Unmarried heterosexual couples account for 2.6 million of these households, while there are an estimated additional 1.6 million same-sex couples. One million children from these households are under the age of 15.

It's also a fact that 75% of us—married or unmarried—die intestate, that is, without a will. Unmarried partners need wills even more than married folks in order to secure choices and legal rights otherwise unavailable to them.

Financial and estate planning is absolutely essential for unmarried couples in long-term relationships. The couple's rights, duties, and obligations to one another at the beginning of the relationship, during the relationship, at breakup, and at death should be spelled out in advance. Estate, gift, and income tax consequences can be disastrous for unmarried partners who have acquired assets, taken on debt or mortgage obligations, or who have businesses or property to be disposed of and divided according to personal wishes and with the minimum possible tax exposure. Young children must also be considered in the event of the death of one of the partners. Sound complicated? Not to worry! You'll understand the basics after you've read this section.

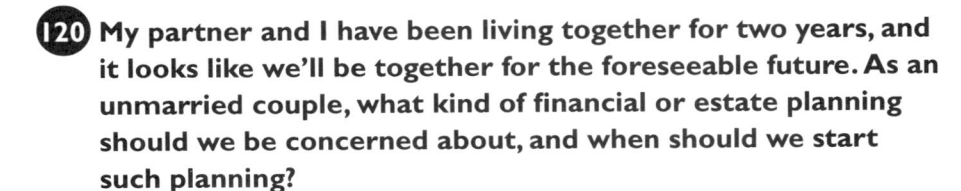

120 My partner and I have been living together for two years, and it looks like we'll be together for the foreseeable future. As an unmarried couple, what kind of financial or estate planning should we be concerned about, and when should we start such planning?

Start early
For unmarried couples, financial planning should begin as soon as the partners start acquiring property and taking on debt. The planning should

focus on the rights, duties, and obligations of each party both during and after the relationship, and should spell out what happens when one partner dies or becomes disabled or mentally incapable of making her or his own decisions.

Even something as innocent as renting an apartment can be a major problem if the couple breaks up. Who leaves and who stays? This may depend on whose name is on the lease, so in this situation both names should probably be on the lease. Partners may also wish to maintain separate checking accounts, separate credit cards, and separate lines of credit, unless the partners don't mind finding themselves liable for one another's debts.

Sharing assets

If the couple is sharing the cost and expense of buying a house, the house should be owned jointly with right of survivorship. This means that regardless of the existence of a will, the property will legally pass to the surviving partner. Special consideration also needs to be given to significant assets which each partner brings to the relationship—such as a business—and to debts and liabilities, including mortgages.

Hot tip!

Such planning, however, is no substitute for a will. Unmarried couples need wills even more than married couples because they cannot rely on the state intestacy laws which apply only to married couples. A will can provide a mechanism to ensure that the wishes of the unmarried partners are carried out, can allow property to pass to the surviving partner, and will also help to protect the survivor from a deceased partner's family who may not have approved of the relationship.

121 Is there anything similar to a prenuptial agreement available to unmarried partners who never intend to marry or cannot marry under state law, such as homosexual couples?

Hot tip!

Yes. It is called a "Living Together Agreement," "No-nuptial Agreement," or "Cohabitation Agreement." Such an agreement enumerates major items purchased together, such as a house, car, or furniture, and how they were acquired. It indicates who is liable for remaining payments upon breakup or death. Such an agreement is similar to a prenuptial agreement for those getting married. To be enforceable, it must be signed voluntarily. The individuals should seek independent counsel and the terms must be fair and reasonable during the relationship and not unconscionable when it ends. The agreement should be entered into as soon as major assets are jointly purchased, especially if there are loans or mortgages present.

The following is a checklist of items that Living Together Agreements should address at each stage of the relationship:

During cohabitation
- *Sharing of living expenses and allocation of incomes*
- *Ownership of assets*
- *Income tax issues: who takes deductions and/or exemptions?*
- *Child support, if applicable*
- *Planning for needs of elderly, ill, or indigent parents*

At breakup
- *Property division—consider property acquired before and during cohabitation. Will joint property be sold?*
- *House or living quarters. Who leaves and who stays? Who retains lease for living quarters?*
- *Mortgages, loans, and other obligations. Who is liable for debts?* Make arrangements for settling of loans between partners.
- *Who pays child support?*

At disability, hospitalization, incompetence, or incapacity
- *Support arrangements*
- *Disability insurance*
- *Living wills, health-care proxies*
- *Medical insurance coverage*
- *Rights of well partner to consume, use, or enjoy property*
- *Rights of ill partner*
- *Consideration of deathbed marriage to gain estate tax advantages or intestacy rights under state law to each other's property*

After the death of either partner
- *Designation of property to be acquired or bequested*
- *Disposition of life insurance proceeds*
- *Disposition of pensions and employee benefits*
- *Disposition of leased property or apartments, or of rent-controlled apartments*
- *Will provisions*
- *Non-probate property transfers (property passing outside the will—see* **Question #210)**
- *Selecting fiduciaries*

Additional protections

Other protective measures include signing a durable power of attorney which will let a partner act on the other's behalf in making financial decisions and signing documents in the event of incapacitation.

Both a living will and a health care proxy should be signed. A living will allows a partner to let his or her health care wishes be known and executed in the event of incapacitation, and the health care proxy allows one partner to make medical decisions for the other if he or she is unable to do so.

Loose ends should be tied up. Beneficiary designations should be changed on insurance policies, IRAs, and company pension plans, especially if there were prior marriages. A new will won't correct this, since beneficiary designations, like joint property ownership, pass outside the will.

Estate and gift tax issues need to be addressed, since there is no marital deduction available to unmarried couples, and they cannot transfer assets without incurring possible gift tax problems.

122 **My partner is afflicted with AIDS, and I have been helping with the payment of the staggering hospital bills. Am I entitled to a deduction for these medical expenses?**

Sadly, this has become a common question. Very often the partner who is healthy wants to help the ill partner with the bills for hospitals, nurses, drugs, and other related medical costs.

If the bills that are not covered by insurance, and need to be paid out-of-pocket, are relatively minor, deductions may not be an issue, because medical expenses must exceed 7.5% of your Adjusted Gross Income (AGI) in order to be deductible. For example, if your AGI is $100,000, then the first $7,500 of medical expenses would not be deductible in any case.

If the bills are high enough to exceed the 7.5% threshold, they are generally only deductible by the partner who incurred the medical expense, unless the medical bills are paid for someone who qualifies as your dependent or "medical dependent," which is usually not the case in these situations. The dependent rules usually apply to parents who deduct medical expenses paid for their children, or to their ill parents who qualify as medical dependents because they have little or no other support.

To qualify as a medical dependent your partner has to satisfy these four tests:

1. Relationship test
To qualify, the person must be your relative or a member of the household. However, if the relationship is in violation your state's laws, you fail this test, as most unmarried couples do.

2. Support test
You must furnish at least half the support for the year. Again, if your partner is employed or receiving severance or other benefits, this test will be tough to pass.

3. Filing status test
Your partner may not file a joint return with a third person. This test is meant to prevent you from claiming your married children or other household members as medical dependents when they file a joint return with their spouse. However, if your partner only files a joint return to get a tax refund and the income test is satisfied, the dependency exemption is allowed.

4. Citizenship test
Your dependent must be a U.S. citizen or a resident of the U.S., Canada, or Mexico.

If your partner qualifies as a medical dependent, then you can deduct medical bills paid on his or her behalf, but you cannot claim him or her as your dependent. (To be considered a full dependent, a partner needs to pass these four tests, and a fifth: his or her income could not exceed the personal exemption limit, which is $2,650 for 1997.) The deduction for medical bills paid for your partner is still limited, though, by 7.5% of your AGI.

Gift tax strategy

Hot tip!

If you cannot get a tax deduction for the medical expenses you paid for your partner, the next best thing is to arrange things so that your partner can get the deduction. The way to do this is with gifting. You're allowed to make tax-free gifts of up to $10,000 per year to as many different individuals as you like. If you give your partner $10,000, and he or she uses it to pay his or her own medical bills, the bills are then deductible on your partner's tax return—again, if they exceed 7.5% of his or her AGI.

In addition to the $10,000 annual gift limit, there is an unlimited gift tax exclusion available to you, the donor, for any amounts paid to providers of medical care for your partner, as long as you make the payment directly to the hospital, doctor, or any institution or individual who provides the medical care for your partner.

123 How should an unmarried couple take title to a home they plan to buy together?

This depends on who is going to pay for the home and the manner in which the couple arranges for the property to be disposed of in the event of a breakup, disability, or death.

If the couple intends to be 50-50 partners all the way, meaning they will each put up half the cash and be equally liable for any mortgage, then it should be held jointly as either joint tenants with right of survivorship (JWROS) or tenants in common.

JWROS means that when one partner dies, the other partner automatically inherits the home. Under tenants in common, on the other hand, when one partner dies, that partner's share goes, not to the other partner, but to his or her own beneficiaries. This is sort of like each partner owning their own half of the house. Of course, the beneficiary may happen to be the other partner. If that's what is desired, then title should be held as joint tenants with right of survivorship as noted above.

If things are not 50-50, and one partner puts up most or all of the cash, then that partner should decide on how the house is owned. If the desire is that this be a joint asset, and thus be titled in joint name, there may be a gift tax problem, since the partner who paid for the house is now gifting a half-share to the other partner. Since the couple is unmarried, they cannot make these transfers gift tax free except for the first $10,000 under the annual gift tax exclusion of $10,000 per person. If the value of the home being transferred from one partner to another amounts to more than $10,000 in any one year, you may want to keep it under the name of the partner who paid for the home until the other partner can buy in.

When both partners contribute to the purchase of the property, careful records must be maintained to determine each partner's individual contribution.

124. What happens to a jointly owned home when the first partner dies?

Jointly owned property (Joint with Right of Survivorship or JWROS) passes to the surviving joint owner, no matter who that joint owner is, and regardless of what a will may say about such property. Joint ownership overrides both wills and trusts that name a beneficiary apart from the joint owner.

However, after the death of the first joint owner, the full value of the entire property may be included in his or her estate if the surviving partner cannot prove his or her share of contributions to the purchase of the home. Since there is no marital deduction available to unmarried partners, an estate tax (which must be paid in cash within nine months) could force the property to be sold if there are no other funds to pay the tax. If the house must be sold to pay estate taxes, any remaining mortgage must be paid off at the time of the sale.

125 **We are an unmarried couple and jointly own a home with a mortgage on it. Who gets the tax deduction for mortgage interest expense?**

Partners can split the loan in any manner that is to their advantage if both partners are named on the mortgage (joint and several liability) and the home or investment property is owned jointly with both partners being named on the title as owners.

If one partner pays all the mortgage interest, then receives repayment from the joint owner for his or her half of that amount, and if the repayment is received in the same tax year, then the joint owners can split the deduction.

However, this is probably not the best way to handle this, since a loan arrangement between the partners, even if short-term, must have repayment terms, collateral, and carry a fair market interest rate to be valid. Otherwise, it may be reclassified as a gift by the IRS. Also, the deduction is more solid if paid directly to the bank. If the joint owners want to split the deduction, 50-50, the best thing to do is for each to pay half. If you do it this way, you won't have to explain the gory details to the IRS.

One partner can gift up to $10,000 a year to the other partner, gift tax free, to help with the payments. Then the joint owner/partner receiving the gift can use the money to pay the mortgage payments directly to the bank, and receive a full tax deduction without any IRS problems.

Tax trap!

If only one partner holds title and is liable on the mortgage, then only that partner may claim the deduction, even if the other partner contributes or pays the mortgage payments in full. In fact, if the other partner does help to pay the mortgage, there may be a gift tax if the total payment exceeds $10,000 in any year.

126 **We are an unmarried couple and own a home jointly. Who gets the deduction for real estate taxes paid on the home?**

Real estate taxes can be split if the home is owned jointly, and then only to the extent that each actually paid the taxes.

127. Could you list the tax benefits that unmarried couples lose by not being married?

Sure:

- *No estate tax marital deduction*

- *No right of election, disinheritance likely* Your spouse can disinherit you, but not easily. And if he or she does, you have a right to elect (thus, the "right of election") to receive a certain amount of property (usually one-third to one-half, depending on your state's laws) from her or his estate.

- *No unlimited tax-free transfers or gifts of property between partners*

- *No legal protection under intestacy provision (when there is no will) which is available to spouses*

- *No joint returns to offset the partners' gains and losses*

Also, at the death of the first partner there may be a federal estate tax if the estate value exceeds $600,000 in 1997, plus applicable state estate taxes. The size of the survivor's estate must therefore be considered. The major concern here is whether or not there will be money to pay estate taxes.

128. What protection is available to children of unmarried partners when the partners both die and leave life insurance money to the children?

The more money, the bigger the fight.

If there is substantial life insurance paid to the minor child or children, there is an increased likelihood of a bitter custody battle pitting the partners' families against one another. Most courts will award custody to a surviving parent, whether married or unmarried, unless it can be shown that the parent is unfit. If there is no surviving parent, however, appointing a custodian to oversee finances and a guardian to care for the children is a crucial matter. The more information in the will regarding reasons for the choice of guardian (religion, moral issues, etc.), the more likely the court will choose the requested guardian. The court is not obligated to follow the will provisions—the childrens' welfare takes precedence.

Section 9
Your Questions About Divorce and Taxes

"If I were your wife, I would put poison in your coffee." Lady Astor
"If you were my wife, I would drink it." Winston Churchill

Divorce is painful enough without having to be a tax expert at the same time. Tax problems with divorce occur most often because important questions are asked too late to help people who will become saddled with disastrous and unexpected consequences. Here are the answers to the tax questions you should ask ahead of time. Believe me, considering these issues early can save a lot of pain later on.

129 My spouse and I are getting a divorce. Is it better to arrange for more of the settlement as child support, or as alimony?

The bottom line is that alimony is deductible to the one who pays it, and counts as income to the one who receives it. Child support, on the other hand, is not deductible to the one who pays it, and does not count as income to the one who receives it.

So if you're paying, you want to pay alimony, and if you're receiving, you want to receive child support.

130 Can I deduct the legal fees of getting a divorce?

No. However, you can deduct fees paid to your lawyer or tax adviser specifically for tax advice, as well as legal fees paid to help you get alimony. As nauseating as it may seem, you should ask your attorney for an itemized bill, stating the amount charged for each of the various services, especially the tax-deductible ones.

131 My spouse and I are divorcing amicably, and we'd like to time the divorce for maximum tax advantage. What is your advice?

The answer depends on whether you both earn about the same income, or one of you is the predominant wage earner.

If you both earn about the same income, you will almost always be better off filing as two single individuals. A December divorce would enable you to do so, since your filing status is based on your marital status on the last day of the year.

However, if one spouse earns most or all of the income, the opposite is true. You should wait until January to get divorced, enabling you to keep filing as a married couple for the previous year (see *Question #112* for more on this).

132. I was married in 1996 and the marriage was annulled in 1997. What is my filing status for these two years?

You're unmarried for both years, since a decree of annulment holds that no valid marriage ever existed. If you already filed a joint return in 1996, you must amend it and file as unmarried, either single or as head of household if you're supporting a child or other relative in your home for more than half the year.

133. I was recently divorced and changed my name. How will this affect my taxes?

If you changed your name because you were divorced or married, you must let both the IRS and the Social Security Administration know.

For the IRS, file Form 8822 "Change of Address." (Even if your address did not change, this is the form to use to report your name change.)

For Social Security, call 1-(800) 772-1213 to find out how to get a new Social Security card. Be prepared to have identification that shows both your old and new names, such as a marriage certificate or a divorce decree. It is essential that the Social Security Administration have the same name in its records that you have on your tax return, because if the IRS cannot match your name to your Social Security number, you'll lose any claimed exemptions and may not receive proper credit for taxes or estimated taxes paid. You also want to make sure the Social Security Administration is correctly crediting your wages to your Social Security account under your proper name.

134. **In 1996 my spouse and I filed jointly and set up estimated tax payments for 1997, which we paid throughout 1997. In 1997, we divorced. How do I get credit for my share of the joint estimated tax payments we made?**

You divide the payments either in half, or in some other manner which you both agree on. If you can't agree on how to split the payments, they will be divided proportionately according to your shares of the 1997 tax. Also, make sure to notify the IRS about the payment-splitting by listing your former spouse's Social Security number on your personal tax return, Form 1040, in the space that you would have used for your ex-spouse's Social Security number if you were filing married.

If you remarried, use your new spouse's Social Security number in the proper place on the form, then go to the second page or the back of Form 1040, and write in the letters "DIV" next to the line which shows your 1997 estimated tax payments and list your share there.

135. **My ex-spouse and I divorced last year, so we are each filing our own tax returns as single individuals this year. How do we report interest income from the joint bank account we had when we were married?**

You should each report half the interest, but it's not simple. The bank will issue Form 1099-INT to both the taxpayer and the IRS, reporting the joint interest earned under either your or your ex-spouse's Social Security number. The spouse whose Social Security number is listed on the 1099-INT form should report the entire amount on Schedule B, then deduct one-half of that interest, also on Schedule B, and write in, "Less interest received as nominee." The other spouse then reports their half on their tax return. You have to go through this to avoid an IRS letter writing campaign that will most likely last longer than your marriage did.

136. **As part of our divorce agreement, I am to receive half of my husband's pension plan at work. Is this pension distribution taxable to me?**

It depends on what you do with the money. If you roll it over to your own IRA account, it's not taxable to you. This should be done subject to what is called a "QDRO," which stands for Qualified Domestics Relations Order. This is an order placed on the plan to make sure you get your share of your former spouse's pension. If it is not rolled over to your IRA, it will be treated as a taxable distribution to you. And, just in case you care, the distribution to you from your ex-spouse's plan will also not be treated as a taxable distribution to him.

137 **I know that because my wife has custody of our child that she is entitled to claim the exemption, even though I pay for my child's support. But I am in a high tax bracket and she's not. Is there a way I can get the exemption since it's probably worth much more to me tax-wise than it is to her?**

Yes, if your spouse consents by filing form 8332, "Release of Claim To Exemption For Child of Divorced or Separated Parents." But don't be so sure that you will get the exemption. Remember: for high income earners, the exemption is phased out (see *Question #67*). It may just turn out that she gets a better tax break on the exemption than you do. Better try it both ways to see which way it works best.

138 **As part of our divorce agreement, my wife has custody of our daughter and claims her as a dependent, but I pay her college tuition. Under the new tax law can I take advantage of the education tax credits?**

No, and your wife can't either. You really blew it tax-wise. To claim either the HOPE Scholarship Tax Credit or the Lifetime Learning Credit (see *Questions #42 and #43*), you must be able to claim your child as a dependent *and* pay the tuition. Since you pay the tuition and your wife takes the child as a dependent, you both lose. This is something new that needs to be figured into child support agreements.

139 **I am divorced and my wife has custody of our children and is entitled to claim them as dependents. However, I am paying high medical bills for my children. Can I deduct these as medical expenses?**

Yes, provided they exceed 7.5% of your Adjusted Gross Income (AGI). Even though you are not the custodial parent, you are entitled to deduct these expenses as long as the child lived with *either* of you for more than half the year and more than half of the child's support came from both of you put together.

140 **In 1996 my spouse required a lot of medical care. In 1997, we divorced but I still paid medical bills from 1996 with checks I wrote in 1997. Can I deduct these as medical expenses?**

Yes. If the bills exceed 7.5% of your Adjusted Gross Income, you are allowed to deduct medical expenses incurred by your former spouse while you were married, but paid after you divorced.

141 **My husband and I divorced over ten years ago. I kept the house, which was worth $150,000 at the time of the divorce, and he received $75,000 in cash. We originally bought the house for $100,000 and it is now worth $250,000. The house is in my name alone and now I want to sell it. How much tax will I owe?**

None! You get to keep the cash. This was the single most common tax trap in the area of divorce, but no more. Gains of $250,000 or less ($500,000 for married couples) on home sales after May 6, 1997 are exempt from capital gains tax (see *Questions #147-#151*).

The new tax law also provides a home sale tax break to the spouse who leaves the home, but retains an ownership interest. If the divorce or separation agreement provides that when the home is sold the two spouses will split the sales proceeds, the spouse who left will also qualify for his or her own $250,000 exclusion, even if the home is sold ten years later and he or she did not live in it the required two years. For the spouse who left the home to qualify, the other spouse must live in the home for two of the five years prior to the sale, and the plan to split proceeds must be stated in the divorce instrument. Each ex-spouse must file for their own $250,000 exclusion as any non-related owner of a home would (to qualify for a joint $500,000 exclusion, you must file a joint return).

By the way, the $75,000 your husband received is 100% tax-free because it's a property settlement.

142 **I am now divorced. What happens if the IRS audits the joint return I filed with my ex-spouse two years ago when we were married, and there are taxes to pay?**

You're both jointly and severally liable for any tax interest and penalties owed on a joint return, even if you're now legally divorced. Joint and several means that the IRS can go after either one of you for the entire amount owed. If one of you skips town, the IRS can go after the spouse that's easier to find and easier to collect from.

143 Can I use the "innocent spouse" rules to protect me from the IRS problems in the question above?

Probably not. So-called "innocent spouse relief" is only available when you can prove that you were unaware of or had no reason to be aware of the activities causing the tax, and did not benefit financially from the unreported income, disallowed or invalid deductions, or credits claimed. How involved you were in the financial affairs in question, and the degree of your education and sophistication will also affect your eligibility for innocent spouse relief. If you do qualify, you may be relieved of the tax liability caused by the "guilty" spouse.

144 What if the divorce decree says that my ex-spouse is solely responsible for the total tax liability on our joint return?

That's not good enough. The IRS is not a party to your "agreement" and is not bound by its terms. However, if you have the resources, you may hire an attorney to enforce the divorce decree on your ex-spouse, assuming she or he has the resources to comply.

145 Following up on the Questions #142-#144 above, this seems so unfair. You mean to say that if my spouse skips town, the IRS won't even bother trying to track him down and will just hit me for the entire amount of back tax owed?

Yes. However, some small amount of progress has been made to resolve this unfair situation. Under the Taxpayer Bill of Rights 2, the IRS is required to let you know that they have made some attempt to collect from the spouse who flew the coop. Although this does not have a lot of teeth, it's a start. But for now, if you make an easier target, don't count on the IRS bending over backward to find your rat of an ex-spouse.

146 **I divorced and then re-married. This year I filed a joint return with my new husband and was due a refund, but since my new husband owed past-due child support to his ex-wife, the IRS applied our entire refund to the money he owed. This doesn't seem fair—he owes the money, not me. Is there anything I can do?**

Yes. Since you do not owe the money, you are entitled to your share of the refund on the joint return you filed with your new spouse. (The IRS considers you an "injured spouse.") Since you have already filed your return, you must fill out IRS Form 8379, "Injured Spouse Claim and Allocation," to claim your share of the refund or overpayment. File it at the IRS center where you filed your original return. To qualify as an injured spouse, you must meet all three of the following requirements:

- *You are personally not required to pay the past due amount that your husband owes*

- *You had your own income—whether from wages, taxable interest, pensions, etc.—which you reported on your joint return, or you live in a community property state (other than Arizona)*

- *You made your own federal tax payments, either through wage withholding or estimated tax payments, or you qualified for a refundable credit, such as the earned income credit.*

Injured spouse relief applies not only to past due child support, but also to spousal support payments or to other federal debts such as student loans. After you file Form 8379, the IRS will figure your part of the overpayment or refund and refund it to you.

If you have not yet filed your return, you may file Form 8379 with your joint return and write "Injured Spouse" in the upper left-hand corner of the return.

Section 10
Your Questions About Your Home and Your Vacation Home

If I were asked to name the chief benefit of the house, I should say: the house shelters day-dreaming, the house protects the dreamer, the house allows one to dream in peace.
   Gaston Bachelard

For many, a home is the largest single asset they will ever own. As such, it's extremely important to manage it wisely, both to keep your nest comfortably feathered, and to ensure your financial future. The new tax law gives homeowners some much-needed relief by eliminating payment of capital gains on most home sales.

But gains are not the full story on home sales. Recent weakness in the real estate market in many parts of the country means that, for many recent buyers of homes, the possibility of suffering a loss when a home is sold is a real possibility. A further complication to the tax picture may come when the home is sold and you have previously elected to take a home office deduction.

(147) **I plan to sell my own home in 1998 at a large profit and move to another part of the country. How will the new tax rules affect me?**

First, my congratulations. Whether by luck or by prophecy, you're picking the right time to sell your home and take a gain, as long as you fulfill the government's requirements. Here's the scoop…

New tax rules on home sales
The Taxpayer Relief Act of 1997 is manna for homeowners who plan to sell their homes. It will exempt most home sales from capital gains tax. The general rules are pretty straightforward, but there are a number of side issues that are important. Here are the basic provisions and the issues and opportunities created by the legislation.

General provisions
Married couples filing jointly can now exclude up to $500,000 ($250,000 for individuals) of gain on homes sold after May 6, 1997. This is not a

once-in-a-lifetime tax break: you can use this exclusion once every two years, no matter what your age.

The requirements are that you must have owned and occupied your home as a principal residence for at least two out of the five years prior to the sale.

Partial exclusions available
Under the new home sale provision you may be allowed a partial exclusion if you do not meet the two-year rule. The three partial exclusions carved out in the new law are for home sales which occurred because of change of place of employment, health problems, or "unforeseen circumstances." However, the IRS has not yet defined "unforeseen circumstances." But we can take as an example the situation where you only lived in your home for one year and then had to move because of your job. Since you were living in the home 50% of the two-year required period, you would be allowed 50% of the ($500,000 if married, $250,000 if single) exclusion.

Losses still not deductible
Unfortunately, the tax package brings no relief here. Losses on home sales are still nondeductible.

No more tainted spouse rule
Under the old $125,000 once-in-a-lifetime exclusion rules, if you married someone who had already taken their $125,000 exclusion, you were considered "tainted" and were no longer eligible for an exclusion since your new spouse had already used theirs. This won't happen under the new law, since the tax break is available an unlimited number of times.

Big profits
Even if your gain exceeds $500,000, there are still tax breaks in the law for you because the gain in excess of $500,000 ($250,000 if single) is taxed at a maximum of only 20% under the new capital gains tax rules (see *Question #28*). And if you acquire the home after the year 2000 and own it for at least five years, that 20% rate will go down to 18%.

Vacation home tax strategy
If you have a vacation home you want to sell, but it would cause a huge tax because it's not your principal residence, you could consider moving

into your vacation home for two years, then selling it. You then would qualify for the $500,00/$250,000 tax break. You could move back into your main home for two years, sell it, and get another $500,000/$250,000 exemption from tax. No tax on either home sale!

Hot tip!

The drawback to this strategy is that if your vacation home is in a different state from your primary home, once you have lived in your vacation home for the two years, you will be considered a resident of that state. This may cause state tax problems for you.

148 I sold my home before the tax law changed. What options are available to me to avoid having to pay a whopping capital gains tax?

Figuring taxes on the sale of your home
If you sold your home before May 7, 1997, you may be subject to capital gains tax if you sold at a profit. The capital gains tax rate can be as high as 28% (plus any state tax), depending on your tax bracket.

The only exception is the $125,000 "once-in-a-lifetime" exclusion for those 55 years old and over, and the two-year rollover rule, which defers, rather than excludes, the gain from tax (see below).

Once in a lifetime $125,000 exclusion (old law)
If you or your spouse are 55 years old or over, you can exclude up to $125,000 of the gain on the sale of your home, but you can use this provision only once during your lifetime. If you have not used it, and then marry someone who already has, you cannot take the exclusion because you have married a "tainted" spouse. Isn't that romantic? You can avoid this problem, though, by marrying someone who waited and saved their exclusion just for you.

The home must also be your principal residence (not a vacation or second home), and the person who was 55 or over must have both owned and lived in the home for at least three out of the five years prior to the date the home was sold. If you're married and the home is not owned jointly, the spouse whose name is on the deed must qualify, and the other spouse must consent to the election. Unmarried couples who own a home jointly each get their own $125,000 exclusion.

If your home is part business (home office or two-family rental), the exclusion is only available to the personal residence portion. It cannot be used against the business part of the gain (see *Question #155*).

Of course, you'll be hearing little about the one-time exclusion in the future because the new tax law supplants it.

Rollovers still a possibility

If you had a gain that exceeded the exemption limits and you sold your home after May 6, 1997, you can still use the old provision allowing you to roll over the gain into a house that cost as much or more as your old home. You must have sold your home or have had a binding contract to sell by August 5, 1997, and you must close on your new home by August 5, 1997. After August 5, 1997, the new rules will be applied and no rollovers will be allowed.

149 **I have already used my once in a lifetime $125,000 exclusion on the sale of my home. Am I still entitled to the $500,000 exemption from tax on the sale of my new home spelled out in the new tax law?**

Yes, as long as the home qualifies under the new rules outlined in *Question #147*.

150 **This new $500,000 tax-free home sales law sounds pretty good, but I have been trading up (buying a new home of equal or greater value) for 30 years and if I sell I'll have a gain of $800,000. What should I do?**

Thank your lucky stars! Even though the $500,000 amount was meant to cover the gain on most home sales, "poor" guys like you will still get a break. Although, if you sell your home after August 5, 1997, you can no longer trade up tax-free by using the old rollover rule (see *Question #148*), you still can exclude the first $500,000 of your profit if you are married filing joint, or $250,000 if you're single. If you've saved your receipts from capital gains improvements made over the years, you can deduct them from any gain above the $250,000/$500,000 exclusions. Any remaining capital gain will be taxed at the new lower maximum capital gains rates (see *Question #28*).

151. Does the new law on capital gains from home sales mean that I'm done saving my receipts for capital improvements?

Although the new law has excluded the profits from most home sales from capital gains tax, you should keep your receipts for improvements, unless you are sure that your home will qualify and that your capital gain will be less than $500,000 ($250,000 if single).

You should definitely keep your receipts for capital improvements on vacation homes, second homes, and rental properties, because these do not qualify for the big exclusion from capital gains. Also, if your gain is more than the exclusion, you will want to add up your improvements to offset any remaining gain. For example, if you're married and have an $800,000 gain, the first $500,000 is exempt if you're married filing joint, but the next $300,000 could be offset by home improvements.

152. I am about to sell my home at a loss. Can I deduct this loss?

No. A loss on the sale of a personal residence is not deductible.

If the property were partly used for business or as a rental (two-family house), then the loss on the business portion would be a deductible capital loss (see *Questions #73 and #155* for more detail on properties used partly for business and partly as personal residences).

153. I am about to sell my home at a loss. After reading Question #152, I know that I cannot deduct this loss, but I would hate to lose it. If, just before I sell it, I turn it into a rental property—which would make this a business property—can I now deduct the loss?

This is obviously a tax motivated transaction, and if that is all that it is, then the IRS will dismiss the whole thing as a sham and you will not be able to deduct the loss.

On the other hand, if there is some substance to the arrangement, then the loss may be deductible, since the loss on the sale of a business (rental) property is deductible. Although your question is a commonly asked one, the switch is, unfortunately, not actually that easy to accomplish.

Let's play out an example. You would have to leave your home without selling it, and move somewhere else to have the full loss be deductible when you sold. Next, you would have to make a good faith effort to rent the home. You would probably want to, anyway, to cover the huge cost of keeping a second home. Now you're a landlord. My congratulations to you, or more appropriately, my sympathies, because the job of landlord is no easy one. Remember: you have to actually go through the motions and walk the walk. You cannot simply call the house a rental property a month before the sale and take the loss as though you had sold a business property.

Since your "loss," if any, is measured from the value at the time you converted the property to a rental or business-use property, any loss which has occurred prior to the conversion would not be deductible. This is why the "take the loss" concept in your question usually does not work out unless you hold on to the property for a long time after you have moved out, and the home continues to decline in value.

You really have to ask yourself whether all this is worth it. The IRS doesn't have fools working for them, and they can spot a phony a mile away. It sounds good, but you're not the first, and surely won't be the last to try it. My best advice is: don't do this unless it is a long-term plan and the loss is substantial enough to make it worthwhile financially. The true long-term tax benefits, if they exist at all, are probably not worth the headaches.

154 I'm thinking about trying to qualify for the home office deduction. Should the new law on capital gains tax for home sales affect this?

Tax trap!

You may be heading for a tax trap if you're going through all the machinations and requirements to turn part of your home into a home office. If you're planning on selling within the next few years, I would advise against it. You will have turned part of your home into a business property and that part will not qualify for the exclusion of gain on home sales because it will no longer be a principle residence. The home office will only benefit you if you're going to use it for the long term or if you're renting.

155 I have been writing off the cost of the part of my home that qualifies for the home office deduction. I am now selling the home at a substantial loss. Can I deduct this loss?

This question raises several tax issues, some of which may surprise and disappoint you. What makes you so sure it's a loss? It may appear to you to be a loss because you know that you're selling the home for less than you paid for it. That sure sounds like a loss to me. However—and it is always the however part that makes people hate the tax laws—for tax purposes you may actually have a taxable gain because of something called "depreciation recapture," which we touched on in *Question #77*. Here is a simplified example of how this works.

Example:

Let's say you bought your home some years ago for $100,000 and are about to sell it for $80,000. So far that sounds like a loss of $20,000. Of course, you cannot deduct the loss on the portion of the structure you use as your home, because the loss on the sale of a personal residence is not deductible. However, this is a partial business property, since you have been using, say, 25% of the house as a home office. Therefore, 25% of the loss, or $5,000, should be deductible, because losses on a business property are deductible, right? Yes and no.

Yes, a loss on the sale of a business property is deductible. But don't be so sure that, as far as the IRS is concerned, there is, in fact, a loss. Let's further assume in our example that $10,000 of depreciation deductions have been taken over the years on the 25% of the home used for business.

You have two sales

For tax purposes, the first thing you must do when selling a property that is used partly for business is to split the sale into two separate sales. The first is a sale of the part that has been used as a residence, and the second is a sale of the part used for business.

Sale of the residence portion: 75%

In our example, 75% of the home is used as a personal residence.

The selling price is .... $60,000 (75% of the $80,000)
The cost is .... $75,000 (75% of the $100,000)
The loss is .... ($15,000)

This is not a deductible loss, because it represents the loss on the sale of a personal residence.

Sale of the business portion: 25%
In our example, 25% of the home is used as a business—your home office.

The selling price is	$20,000 (25% of the $80,000)
The cost is	$25,000 (25% of the $100,000)
The loss is	($5,000)

This would be a deductible loss if this were the end of the story, but it isn't.

You must now reduce your loss (or add to your gain, if there was a gain) by the $10,000 of depreciation taken over the years. From the government's point of view, you have already deducted this amount, so why should they let you deduct it again by letting you use your original cost? The IRS will require that you reduce your cost by the amount of depreciation you have deducted in past years. In our example, this would mean that the cost you would use for calculating gain or loss on the business portion is your original cost of $25,000 (25% of $100,000), less the depreciation claimed of $10,000. Now your cost for tax purposes is $15,000. If your selling price is $20,000 (25% of the $80,000) and your cost is $15,000, you have arrived at a taxable gain of $5,000.

Now, back to the answer to your question. Using the numbers in our example, you have a personal loss of $15,000 on the portion used as your personal residence, which is not deductible, and you have a $5,000 taxable gain on the business portion. Just when you're down about "losing" money on the sale of your home, they further kick you by turning it into a profit on which you now owe tax. To pour more salt on your wounds, the tax you pay on the gain in this example is paid at the new maximum 25% rate on depreciation recapture on business real estate sales after May 6, 1997, unless your tax bracket is lower, in which case you pay that rate. Depreciation recapture is not granted the favorable capital gain tax rates because the IRS feels that you deducted it all these years at ordinary rates, so why shouldn't you pay it back that way?

However, if the gain exceeds the amount of depreciation taken—in our example, $10,000—then that excess is taxable at capital gains tax rates.

Bad tax law

Let's assume that the gain on the business portion of the home was $30,000. Then the first $10,000 (the depreciation recapture) will be taxed at 25% and the next $20,000 of gain will taxed as a capital gain.

Depreciation recapture at ordinary income tax rates applies mainly to depreciable property placed in service before 1987. Homes or buildings (real property) depreciated under the method called MACRS (Modified Accelerated Cost Recovery), in effect for buildings placed in service after 1986, are subject to recapture at capital gains tax rates. For sales after May 6, 1997, the new 25% rate applies. Go figure. The good news is: if you rent, none of this applies to you!

It should be noted that our example was overly simplified so that you can understand the mechanics of the tax law when it comes to the sale of a part business, part personal property. We did not include improvements to the property or add in closing costs and adjustments when you buy and sell the home. These should always be figured into the equation.

156 Regarding the question above, can I avoid the depreciation recapture tax trap by simply not claiming the depreciation deductions? After all, if I do not deduct it, I do not have to add it back when I sell, right?

Wrong. Heads they win, tails you lose. If you were entitled to take depreciation deductions but did not—whether by design, forgetfulness, or ignorance—you still must recapture the depreciation deductions that you could have taken but did not. You'd better use the depreciation deductions: you'll not only lose them if you don't, but the IRS will take them back when you sell, whether or not you took them.

Really stupid tax law

Remember: the recapture provisions (at ordinary income tax rates) for homes or buildings do not apply to property placed in service after 1986, but you still must reduce your basis (your original cost plus improvements) by the amount of depreciation you were allowed to deduct, whether you did so or not.

157 My taxes are too high. Should I buy a second home for the tax advantages?

No. Classic mistake. You're investing for the wrong reasons. No matter what you have heard about a second home, it is almost never a tax shelter.

It is usually a money pit, partially financed by the government through write-offs for mortgage interest, real estate taxes, depreciation, and annual losses incurred in renting the home out. While it may seem that you're reducing your taxes, you're also reducing your cash because you're spending it. You get a tax deduction by spending money on tax-deductible items. Would you give all your money to charity, just so you'd owe no taxes?

Most people buying a home for tax reasons really want a second home as a private getaway in the country or an apartment in the city for weekends, and are rationalizing their decision to buy by thinking it's a good "tax shelter." Some people like to imagine that it is an "investment." Most times it is neither. The only way to possibly benefit, tax-wise and investment-wise, from a second home is to treat it as a business, which means renting it out most of the time. That's probably not what you had in mind, is it? You want to use it and enjoy it. Then do it! But not for tax reasons.

Tax trap!

Vacation/second home could create estate tax obligation
If you do buy a second home or vacation home, and it is located in a different state from the one in which you are currently a resident, then, when you die, that state may make a claim on part of your estate, depending on how much time you have spent at the second home. You may also be subject to ancillary probate (a second probate in the state where your vacation home is located—see *Question #217* for details).

Vacation/second home insurance problem
If you spend too much time away from your primary residence, you may jeopardize your homeowner's coverage if damage or theft occurs while you're away. Policies typically have a clause denying coverage if you abandon your home, with "abandoment" usually defined as an absence of 30 days or more.

158 **What are the tax benefits of renting out a second home? Does it pay?**

As I said in *Question #157*, there are only benefits if you treat it as a business, which means limiting your personal use to 14 days a year, or to no more than 10% of the number of days it is actually rented at a fair rental value, whichever is greater. If you go beyond these personal use limits, the property will be treated as either a personal or "mixed-use" (part personal, part business property) rather than a business-use property. You may rent your home for up to 14 days a year without having to report any of the rent as income, but then you cannot deduct any rental expenses.

Keep it business

Let's assume that you're serious and plan to use the second home as a business property. One of the factors that should obviously go into your decision to buy is profit. You're not investing to lose money in the name of current tax benefits. You should be investing in a home or property that you feel has good long-term appreciation potential. Remember, this is not a vacation house anymore. It is an investment—and investments are meant to go up in value. Making a profit is your first concern, not tax benefits. You will receive the tax benefits anyway, so why not get them on the best possible investment property?

Qualifiying for the business-use tax benefits

The tax benefits only apply to business-use properties, so watch out for the 14 day rule—you must limit your personal use as noted above. The major benefit is the deduction for annual rental losses, subject to the passive loss rules on deductibility. The rental losses consist of rental-related deductions that exceed the rental income. The allowable deductible expenses are items like: mortgage interest and real estate taxes, repairs and maintenance, management fees or rental commissions, maintenance charges (for condos and coops), legal and other professional fees, utilities, insurance, advertising, depreciation, and travel expenses or trips to check up on the property and resolve any tenant problems.

If you use your home personally for more than the 14 days, and rent it out for more than 14 days, you have "mixed-use" property (part personal and part business property) and the full tax benefits are lost because rental expenses can only be deducted from rental income, and cannot be used to reduce other forms of taxable income. Thus, if expenses exceed your rental income in any given year, they may not be deducted in that year, but must be carried forward to future years when the property shows a profit. Also, with mixed-use property, the rental deductions must be allocated between personal and business use. Mortgage interest, real estate taxes, and casualty losses are still fully deductible, but other expenses which are allocated to personal use are not.

Special tax benefits if you manage yourself

If you actively manage the property yourself, and most people do, you may be able to deduct from your regular income up to $25,000 a year in rental losses. This also includes a two-family or multi-unit dwelling. Active management means that you're involved in decisions about repairs and maintenance, hiring workers or contractors, and setting the rent or lease terms. Even if you hire an agent to handle these issues for you, you can still qualify as actively managing if you reserve control and are consulted on decisions about the property, tenants, and rental rates. If you do qualify as actively managing the property, the average rental period must be more than seven days. If weekly rentals are the rule, then make sure that the home is rented for at least one longer period so that the average rental period is greater than seven days.

$25,000 rental loss deduction limitation

However—and this is the last however—even if you qualify under the tests above, the $25,000 limit phases out as your Adjusted Gross Income (AGI) exceeds $100,000 (the $25,000 rental loss is reduced by $1 for every $2 by which your income exceeds the $100,000). Thus, when AGI hits $150,000, you no longer may deduct the losses on your current tax return. They are not lost, but go into a large black hole of tax law called "suspended losses from passive activities." These losses may be carried over to future years when your AGI is under $150,000, when the property shows a profit, or when you sell or dispose of the property. At these points, the accumulated losses are no longer suspended, and can be used to offset a gain on the sale, or, if you sell at a loss, they may be deducted.

14 day tax-free income

The other tax benefit, if you decide to use the property as a second home and do not pass the business use tests, is that mortgage interest (on up to $1.1 million of combined mortgage and home equity debt for both your primary and second homes) and real estate taxes are deductible. You can still rent your vacation home—and this goes for your primary residence as well—for up to 14 days without having to report the rental income.

159 What qualifies as a second home?

Practically anything that is livable, meaning that it has sleeping and bathroom facilities. This can include a boat, trailer, apartment, motor home, condo, coop, or even a garage.

Section 11
Your Questions About Your Audit

Some men will rob you with a six-shooter, some with a fountain pen.
  Bob Dylan

The seven most feared words in America are "Your return has been selected for examination."

Yes. This means that you're about go through a tax audit. While never a pleasant experience, it does not have to be equated with torture. This section will help prepare you and will give you important tips for making it through the audit process unscathed. Not knowing what you're up against in life is often the biggest reason for anxiety. So you'll know what you'll be facing if the IRS decides to drop by, here are the audit basics:

160 What are the odds my return will be selected by the IRS for an audit?

Oh, if only I (or anyone else) knew the answer to this question, I wouldn't be sitting here writing this book. And if I did know, and still wrote this book, you couldn't afford it, because there would only be one copy and I would auction it off at Sotheby's.

The way the IRS letter starts with the words, "your return has been selected," it almost sounds as if you've won the lottery. In fact, the chances are about as great; the odds of being selected for a tax audit are just over 1%. The chances of being "selected," though, are much greater when your return reflects big deductions or losses, or contains errors or other inconsistencies. Self-employed individuals filing Schedule C with incomes exceeding $100,000 probably stand the greatest audit risk of all, possibly as high as one in twenty. Your risk also depends on your geographic location and the types of deductions you claim. The IRS actually scores each tax return, using computers to generate statistics and comparisons. One thing we do know is that the higher your income, the greater your chances are of being selected for audit.

161 Are there really "red flags" that will trigger an audit?

Yes. Although many of the factors the IRS uses to decide who to audit are top-secret, here are five important ones:

Unreported income

This is probably the single biggest area that flags returns for audit. It is done by computer matching programs that compare your returns to IRS information on your Social Security number and, if you have a business, your federal Employer Identification Number (EIN). There is so much that the IRS already knows about your income that it is dangerous to leave anything out, whether through honest error, sloppiness, or in the ridiculous hope that they won't find out about it.

Tax trap!

Your income information is provided to the IRS by the people who pay you money, through W-2 forms for wages and 1099 forms for income from items such as interest, dividends, real estate rentals, retirement plan distributions, lottery and gambling winnings, sales of stocks and bonds, tax refunds, and even from the sale of your home. If you're self-employed, there is a good chance that much of your business income is already on file with the IRS, whose computers are just waiting to kick your return out if you have failed to report any income.

Phony dependents

Tax trap!

There were over seven million dependents that mysteriously disappeared from tax returns several years back, when Congress decided that taxpayers who claim dependents should not only list the Social Security numbers of those dependents, but also state their first and last names. Even with this crackdown, people still list their pets and their children who no longer live with them, or who never existed in the first place. The IRS also looks at returns for how many dependents are claimed. For example, a couple with $15,000 in income who list 12 dependents will most likely be hearing from Uncle Sam, just to check up on the family. Fake dependents are easily caught by the IRS these days, so leave your pets and imaginary friends off your return.

High deductions

Even if the deductions are legitimate, if they appear high in relation to your reported income, your return could be flagged. Attaching documentation to your return explaining the large tax deductions could help prevent an audit. This is particularly helpful with high medical or contribution deductions, or with super-sized casualty or theft losses. For example, if you had a huge casualty loss from a hurricane, you should explain the nature of the damages and note the date or add a statement that the President has declared your area a Federal Disaster Area.

Deductions that appear to be overstated will light up the IRS's computers. This is especially true for business deductions, including meals and entertainment, a pet peeve of the IRS. Omitting required documentation for charitable contributions, especially for non-cash contributions that should be listed on Form 8283, "Noncash Charitable Contributions," increases the chances of an audit.

Sloppy returns with mistakes
If you're doing your returns by hand, make sure you're filling the forms out correctly and putting the information on the correct lines. Write legibly. Many returns are selected for audit simply because they are a mess or are riddled with arithmetic errors. If you're preparing your own return, make sure that you really know what you're doing, and that you check it or have someone else check it before filing it.

Hobby losses
If you're taking large losses from an activity that appears to have no profit motive, the IRS will want to find out more about your "business" and will check to see that you're not just investing in your hobby. If you do not show a profit in at least three of five consecutive years, the IRS will call it a hobby unless you can clearly prove that there is a serious intent to earn a profit. This is not an easy case to win, so be careful and keep good records. If your activity ends up being deemed by the IRS to be a hobby, you may only deduct expenses to the extent that the hobby generates income.

162 What if I do get a letter telling me I've been selected for audit?

So what? The first thing to do is relax. It's only an audit, not a death sentence. But don't ignore the notice, since doing that will only make things more stressful in the long run. If you had a CPA or tax professional prepare your return, call him or her, or send the notice. He or she will guide you. If you did the return yourself, read the notice carefully to find out exactly what type of audit it is.

What type of audit is it?
The notice will either ask you to make an appointment to visit the IRS (an office or desk audit) or to come and see you at your home or business (a field audit). A field audit is the more serious of the two. During such

an audit they will be questioning more items and may even want to have a "look around." If you're worried or uncomfortable with a house call, you may want to call in a tax pro to represent you, even if you did not have your return prepared by one.

163 What should I do first to get ready for the audit?

After you have decided on whether you will represent yourself or hire someone, contact the IRS agent or appointment clerk named in the letter and set up an appointment with them. Make sure that you leave yourself enough time to properly and thoroughly prepare. First impressions count, especially at a tax audit. Do not feel pressured to agree to the audit date that the IRS gives you or to a date that you know does not leave you ample time to present your case. You will only end up having to cancel and that looks worse.

Be prepared!
This old Boy Scout motto works well with the IRS. The key to success at any tax audit is preparation and organization. Once the audit begins, it's too late to go back and make your records look better or clean things up. The tax agent has already seen how you keep records and will make a mental note of it, especially if you keep sloppy files.

Good preparation can bring out both the strengths and weaknesses of your return. Knowing your strong arguments will help you capitalize on them and establish credibility with the auditor. The tax agent is human too. Strong arguments and well-organized records will help carry your weaker arguments. The agent will look at you differently once he or she sees you as someone who takes your taxes seriously.

On the other hand, shoddy or disorganized records will probably influence the IRS to question more items until they can satisfy themselves about whether or not your proof is adequate. They don't want to deal with a mess—dumping a pile of papers on their desk can only hurt you, and can make them a little more skeptical about everything else. If the agent becomes really suspicious, they can open up other tax years for audit, as well as pry more deeply into your return.

Build up your case

Another benefit of good audit preparation is that it enables you to correct weaknesses well before the tax agent ever sees them. For example, if you're being asked to prove charitable contributions and you have questionable documentation, you will have time to find or acquire the receipts and/or canceled checks you need to make your case. Then, when the agent asks you for the proof, you can pull it out and end the discussion of the issue. This establishes instant credibility, and, believe me, credibility is essential.

If you're not prepared for a question, you'll have to start fumbling nervously through a pile of papers or end up saying something like, "May I get back to you on that?" The agent usually has no problem with such a request, but two negative developments occur. First, you may have unnecessarily prolonged the audit for at least one more session, and second, you put a question in the agent's mind as to whether you really have the documentation requested. When and if you do finally produce your proof, it will be looked at more closely. You have made the tax agent suspicious.

Such a problem can be avoided with advance preparation. Even if you find that you do not have needed receipts, at least you'll know this in advance, and you'll have time to come up with them or with some other strategy. You'll maintain your credibility with the agent by having answers or explanations ready when you're asked. If you have good answers for the agent's questions, he or she will never know, or care, how long it took you to put them together. In fact, he or she will appreciate that you have made their job easier by not wasting their time and trying their patience.

164. What happens if I am not satisfied with the audit result or cannot see eye to eye with the IRS agent?

Don't worry, be happy! Their word is not final. After all, you're not Leona Helmsley or Al Capone, and you're not going to jail. This is America. Even convicted murderers get to appeal their cases—and so can you.

Only major issues (in dollars) should go to appeals. You do not want to end up paying more in representation fees than the amount of tax in question. If you're going to the appeals level, find out if your representative is experienced with the appeals process. This may be the time to hire someone who can go the distance—through the appeals process and then to Tax Court if necessary. Most audits, however, end at the agent level, well before the appeals and Tax Court phases.

165. What can I do to prevent the IRS agent from disallowing deductions on my return? Don't they have to find something in order to earn their keep?

Contrary to public opinion, no. Of course there will always be overzealous tax agents, but most will be reasonable if you're well-prepared and organized. And yes, there is such a thing as a no-change audit where the IRS accepts your return as filed. I am happy to say that I have had the pleasure of experiencing no-change audits on several occasions, and of even finding additional deductions resulting in a refund for my clients.

How to make your deductions stick

Your success at an audit depends largely on how well you can substantiate your deductions. This takes time, preparation, and organization.

Whether you're representing yourself or hiring an accountant, you should give yourself enough time to neatly organize your records. They should be arranged in a manner that makes it easy for the agent to find whatever he or she needs.

Organizing your records

Start by listing the items or categories that are being examined. The audit letter will tell you which items they want to check. Work on one item at a time. First go to your return and see how much of a deduction you claimed. For example, if you're being questioned about business meals and entertainment (a common request), see how much you deducted. If the amount is $1,482, you know what you need to be able to prove.

Start with the places from which the item would most likely be paid. Your checking account is a good place to start. Then go to your credit card statements or actual credit card receipts if you have them. The next place might be receipts collected when you paid cash. Put them all in order and add them up. If you find that you only came up with $1,160 of the $1,482, then you know exactly how much more you need.

Try to remember meals and entertaining that you may have paid cash for but did not write down. Even if you have no proof, write it down now. To the best of your memory, write down the estimated amount you spent, the type of expense, where the meeting or event took place, which business associates were present, what business was discussed and the approximate date it all took place. Maybe you even picked up a business card of one of the people attending or a matchbook from the restaurant. You might also have a photograph that was taken there. Keep these things and attach them to your written summary of the expenses. If this can account for say, $300 of the $322 you're still looking to account for, you're practically home free. You can even write down that the remaining $22 was an estimated amount.

Put all this together neatly in either a clipped stack or a separate envelope and place a blank cover page on top that says "Meals and Entertainment Deductions for 1996—Total $1,482." Any tax agent will be impressed with this kind of documentation.

This process of organizing should be repeated with each item or category being questioned. Approach the task methodically, chipping away at each item until you're ready to face the tax agent or to hand it off to the professional representing you.

If your accountant sees the kind of preparation you have done, he or she will feel much more confident at the audit. It should take less time, and the tax agent will also be less likely to further question your representative about the items for which you may have no receipts but do have detailed explanations.

If you are up against the agent yourself, you will still be a target for further questioning, because you will be expected to be able to explain your documentation. Your accountant can easily say, "Here's all the documentation and explanations for these deductions, and these are the figures I used to prepare this return." Your tax pro knows how to keep the discussion to a minimum. Taxpayers tend to get nervous and too "chatty" when they represent themselves.

You're responsible

The organization and preparation is your job. These are your records and every person is responsible for their own tax return. Be prepared with an explanation for everything being questioned.

It may even come out that you cheated yourself and that you're entitled to more deductions than you actually claimed. If, in preparing for the audit, you find that you actually have more deductions than you claimed, that's fine. Write them down and the tax agent should allow them or at least use them to offset weaker arguments. You may even be due a refund!

166. Should I hire a tax pro to handle my audit for me, or should I try to represent myself?

Do you consider yourself a match for the IRS? Do you know what not to say? Do you know what to expect at an audit? If you can answer these questions with a secure "Yes," then you may be able to represent yourself and save the professional fees.

Hot tip!

Generally speaking, though, a tax audit is best left in the hands of an experienced tax pro. Your tax preparer is probably your best bet. He or she knows how they compiled the information you provided and are aware of the strengths and weaknesses of your return. If you're not sure whether your tax preparer is the best person to represent you, ask him or her about their audit experience and track record. Also see if you can agree on what you both consider a successful audit result. Find out how long it will take to complete the audit and how much it will cost you to be represented. The answers to the last two questions should not be vague. With appropriate organization and preparation, the average office audit should take no more than one or two visits with the tax agent. Anything longer may indicate poor preparation or an unresolved difference of opinion with the tax auditor, which may necessitate going to appeals.

167. What are the worst mistakes I can make in an audit if I represent myself?

Hot tip!

Talking too much. Tax agents are very experienced and know when to keep their mouths shut—and you should keep yours shut as well. Only answer the questions that are being asked, nothing more. If you don't know the answer or are unsure, simply say, "I'll get back to you on that." That's one of the reasons you may want a tax professional to represent you. It's very easy for them to say, "I'll have to find out about that, I really don't know." It's a little harder for you to say that about your own affairs.

Section 12
Your Questions About Your Pensions and IRAs

I advise you to go on living solely to enrage those who are paying your annuities. It is the only pleasure I have left.
  Voltaire

IRAs and pensions are regulated by the most complex legislation ever enacted in America—and probably anyplace else. There are literally thousands of rules covering pages and pages of regulations practically written in Sanskrit. You would need the patience of a Biblical scholar to get through it, yet you're expected to understand and apply these laws correctly or suffer the consequences—usually in the form of penalties measured in your hard-earned dollars.

Many folks think that IRAs only cover the $2,000 a year you can contribute to your retirement. But it also applies to so much more, including: the new Roth IRA, 401(k), and 403(b) plans, defined benefit plans, money purchase plans, defined contribution plans, Keogh plans, SEP plans, and SIMPLE plans. Funds from many of these will end up in your IRA rollover account when you change jobs or when you retire. So when I talk about IRAs in this section I'm referring to all of these types of tax-deferred plans covered by what is known as the "IRA Distribution Rules," unless I say otherwise. So here goes...

168 By what date must I make my IRA contributions?

By the due date of the return, or April 15 of the year after the year you're paying taxes on. There are no extensions. This is confusing because other plans have different due dates. For example, with a SEP (Simplified Employee Pension), you have until the tax filing date, including extensions. Keoghs must be set up by December 31, but you have until the tax filing date, including extensions, to make a contribution. Congress tried to make this as confusing as possible, and this is the best they could do...for now.

169 What is the new "Roth IRA?"

Beginning in tax-year 1998, a new nondeductible "Roth" IRA, named for Senate Finance Committee Chairman William V. Roth, Jr., will be avail-

New tax law will affect future returns

able. The following are the basics of Roth IRAs:

- *Contributions are not deductible*

- *Eligibility is limited by income, phasing out for singles between $95,000 and $110,000, and for those filing married joint between $150,000 and $160,000*

- *Withdrawals are tax-free if made at or after 59½ years of age and if the funds invested have been held for at least five years (withdrawals from traditional IRAs under these circumstances are taxable)*

- *You may withdraw the principal—the amount you have actually invested—at any time and for any reason without paying penalties or taxes*

- *Being an active participant in your company's plan does not make you ineligible to contribute to a Roth IRA (as it would for a traditional IRA)*

Roth: the King of IRAs

You can still have a traditional IRA if you want it, but if you're eligible for a Roth, why would you want it? The new Roth IRA wins hands down. Whatever way you fund your various IRAs, the maximum total annual IRA contributions made cannot exceed $2,000 a year ($4,000 for couples), and you must have earned income of at least the amount you contribute. The one exception to this rule is the new Education IRA. After you've contributed $2,000 to your IRAs, you may still contribute an additional $500 to an Education IRA for each child who qualifies (See *Question #42* for more on Education IRAs).

Converting your traditional IRA to a Roth IRA

Beginning in 1998, taxpayers with incomes of $100,000 or less may convert an existing IRA to a new Roth IRA. To convert, you must pay income tax on the entire amount that you withdraw from your traditional IRA, but the amount that's converted does not count as income toward the $100,000 limit on income allowable if you're converting. If you convert before January 1, 1999, then you get to spread the income over four years. If you file married separate, however, you cannot convert.

170 Should I pay tax now to convert my existing IRA to a Roth IRA? And should I have an traditional IRA or a Roth IRA?

Here are the factors to consider:

- *Your age* The younger you are, the more years you'll have to benefit from tax-free accumulations, and the greater the tax benefits when you finally begin withdrawing money from your Roth IRA.

- *Your tax bracket* A conversion to Roth can push you into a higher bracket even over the four years that the IRS will give you to pay the tax if you convert before January 1, 1999. On the other hand, in the future on the receiving end, tax-free distributions will be of relatively greater benefit to a retiree who is lucky enough to be in a high income tax bracket. Converting might pay, especially if you have high expenses or a net operating loss carryover from your business that can be used to lessen the tax impact of conversion.

- *Tax payments* The income tax you'll have to pay on the converted funds should be paid out of your non-IRA savings if at all possible. Although you can pay the tax out of your converted funds, if you do so, you'll be reducing the nest egg which would have otherwise grown tax-free. And if you're less than 59½ years old, then you will also be hit with the 10% penalty for early withdrawal, but *only* on the amount not converted to the Roth IRA.

Hot tip!

- *Eligibility for deductibility of contributions* The Roth IRA is ideal for you if you can't make deductible IRA contributions because your income is too high, or if you and/or your spouse are covered by company plans (see *Question #182* for details).

- *Estate planning considerations* The Roth IRA works well if you want to ease the income tax burden on beneficiaries (other than a spouse) who are going to get hit with both an estate tax and income tax. Although they'll still have to pay estate tax, the Roth IRA would eliminate income tax obligations. Similarly, a Roth IRA can provide a surviving spouse beneficiary with completely tax-free income since estate tax is not an issue here.

- *Cash availability* If you have a cash shortage which would make a nondeductible IRA contribution impossible, the traditional deductible IRA is for you, because you'll get a tax deduction which will reduce your outlay for the contribution.

- *Flexibility* The Roth IRA has no rule about mandatory distributions beginning at age 70½, and you can even continue to contribute to a Roth IRA after reaching this age, provided you have sufficient earned income. Also, the way the law is now written, you can pull

Good tax law

out your original contributions at any age without either a penalty or tax. Thus you could make a transfer from a traditional IRA to a Roth IRA, and then remove all the transferred principle tax-free without paying the 10% penalty. Beware: most seasoned observers predict Congress will close this loophole.

- *Future shock* The one thing we know about the future is that it's going to be different from whatever your favorite expert is predicting. Will you be in a high tax bracket or a low one when you retire? What is Congress going to do with income tax rates over the next few years—or decades? Will they re-enact an excise tax on large IRA withdrawals and apply it to Roth IRA distributions? If you think you know the answer to any of these questions, it could affect your decision to go Roth.

(171) **I've heard that there are special circumstances under which I can make withdrawals before age 59½ from my IRAs without paying tax or penalties. What are they?**

New tax law will affect future returns

Good tax law

Oh, I was afraid you were going to ask me that question! This is complicated, so make sure you read my answer fully.

Penalty free? "Yes!" Tax-free? "Maybe..."
Beginning in 1998, you will be able to make *penalty-free* withdrawals from *either* a Roth or traditional IRA in the following circumstances:

- *Up to a $10,000 lifetime maximum for first-time homebuyers*
- *For education*
- *When you're disabled*
- *By a beneficiary of an IRA of someone now deceased*

The only withdrawals that you can make from a Roth IRA before age 59½ that will be *tax-free* (as well as penalty-free) are those which represent principal—what you have actually paid in. You'll have to pay tax on any withdrawals of earnings, with some exceptions (see *Question 173* and the table in Appendix B for information on tax and penalties related to withdrawals from both traditional and Roth IRAs).

172 **Exactly whose and what type of education expenses are eligible for the penalty-free, and in some cases tax-free, IRA withdrawals you mention in Question #171 above?**

Beginning in 1998, there will no longer be a 10% penalty for IRA withdrawals made before 59½ years to pay for higher education expenses for you, your spouse, your children, or even your grandchildren. And your child does not have to be your dependent to qualify for this break. Eligible education expenses include tuition, fees, books, supplies, room and board, and equipment.

New tax law will affect future returns

The break only applies to IRA withdrawals made after 1997 that are used to pay education expenses incurred after 1997. However, this education exception doesn't apply if you use your IRA to pay for education expenses that are effectively reduced by scholarships, veteran's benefits, or redemptions of U.S. Savings Bonds.

In some cases, withdrawals to pay for education, if made from a Roth IRA, may be tax as well as penalty-free. See *Question #173* and the table in Appendix B for more information on taxes and penalties related to withdrawals from both traditional and Roth IRAs.

173 **Is the Roth IRA free of both taxes and penalties if I use its proceeds to pay for education or my first home, or if I'm disabled?**

This is a confusing new area of tax law that has been created just in case the old IRA rules were not complicated enough for you. Before you withdraw money from a Roth IRA under the circumstances you've mentioned, here's what you need to know:

New tax law will affect future returns

As I have mentioned before, the original nondeductible contributions made to the Roth IRA may be withdrawn at any time, for any reason, tax and penalty-free. However, once you start to withdraw the earnings on your contributions, you must pay tax if the withdrawal is made before you are 59½ years old and if the funds have not been held in the Roth IRA for at least five years. The first distributions from Roth IRAs will be considered your principal, that is, as coming from your own nondeductible contributions; subsequent withdrawals will be from earnings on your contributions and will generally be taxable (see Appendix B) unless taken after age 59½ and held for at least five years.

Good tax law

The new tax break is that you will no longer be hit with the 10% penalty for an early withdrawal made for education, first home-buying up to $10,000 lifetime, if you're disabled, or if you're an IRA beneficiary. These exceptions apply to traditional—not just Roth—IRAs beginning in 1998.

Roth IRA withdrawal examples
Example #1
It's the year 2008. You're 55 years old and have contributed a total of $20,000 to your Roth IRA, which is worth $24,000. Let's assume that you want to withdraw $10,000 for your child's college tuition, for your first home, or because you're disabled. The first distributions will be considered your principal, that is, as coming from your own nondeductible contributions. Subsequent withdrawals will be considered to come from earnings. So, in this example, you could have withdrawn up to $20,000 or the total of your own contributions—remember, you wanted $10,000—and have no tax to pay because you did not cut into the $4,000 of earnings. Result: you can take the $10,000 tax and penalty-free.

Example #2
Now let's use the same facts as in the example above, except let's say that you need the entire account, all $24,000, for your child's tuition (this amount exceeds the $10,000 lifetime maximum for first-time homebuyers, so I've left this option out of this example). The entire withdrawal is penalty-free, but it is not all tax-free. In this case, the first $20,000, your own nondeductible contributions, can be withdrawn tax and penalty free, but the last $4,000, considered your earnings, is taxable because you are less than 59½ years old. The education exception relieves you of the 10% penalty, but not the obligation to pay taxes. Result: you'll owe tax on an additional $4,000 in income.

Example #3
Again, let's use the same facts as in the examples above, except this time let's say you're 60 years old and the year is 2013 when you make your withdrawal. The entire withdrawal is now tax and penalty free, not because it's for education, but because you have held the account for at least five years and are more than 59½ years old, had you not the made the withdrawal.

Although in this example you may use the entire account in any way you wish without tax or penalty, it may not be a wise investment move because you will be forfeiting future tax-free growth the account would have produced.

See the table in Appendix B for information on tax and penalties related to withdrawals from both traditional and Roth IRAs.

174 I am buying my first home. If I have both a traditional and a Roth IRA, must I withdraw from the new Roth IRA to avoid the 10% penalty?

No. The new tax law effective beginning in 1998 exempts first-time homebuyers who are under 59½ years old from the 10% early withdrawal penalty on up to $10,000 lifetime maximum of IRA distributions when the distributions are used to purchase or construct a first home. This provision, which is similar to the provision allowing penalty-free distributions for education, is available to all IRAs.

Good tax law

However, you might want to use the Roth IRA if you did not want to pay tax on the withdrawal, since distributions from a Roth IRA are penalty-free (and in some cases, tax-free, too) if used for a first home or education (see the examples in *Question #173* and the table in Appendix B). Remember: these IRA penalty exceptions do not apply until 1998.

175 I want to buy a home. I don't have an IRA —or any savings— but Mom and Pop do. Can my parents tap their IRA, penalty-free to pay for my first home?

Yes, and your grandparents can, too. But do me favor, get a job!

176 My husband and I are buying our first home. Can we double the $10,000 limit to $20,000 by withdrawing the $10,000 maximum from each of our respective IRAs?

Smart guys! The tax provision going into effect in 1998 does not get specific on whether this is per individual, so it appears that you may. Don't show this to those killjoys at the IRS who will try to get Congress to plug this great loophole.

Hot tip!

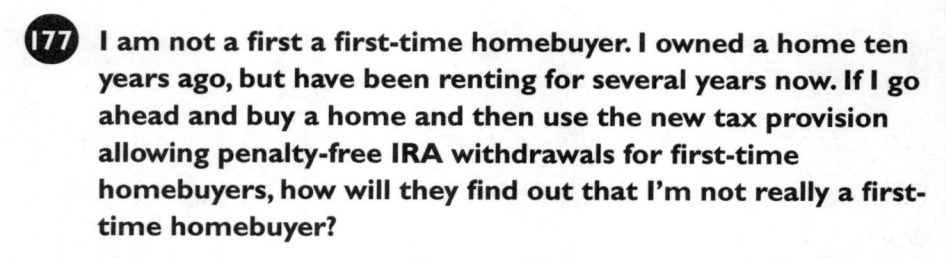

177 **I am not a first a first-time homebuyer. I owned a home ten years ago, but have been renting for several years now. If I go ahead and buy a home and then use the new tax provision allowing penalty-free IRA withdrawals for first-time homebuyers, how will they find out that I'm not really a first-time homebuyer?**

Good tax law

They don't care, because you qualify under the government's definition of a new homebuyer. A well-buried part of this new tax law provision qualifies you as a first-time homebuyer if you have not owned a home for the two years before you buy your new home. If you're married, your spouse must also have not owned a home for the two-year period before you acquire your new home. So don't marry anyone who will blow this tax break for you.

178 **If I withdraw $10,000 from my IRA to buy a first home but the deal goes sour, what am I supposed to do with the $10,000? Can I put it back in my IRA without a penalty?**

New tax law will affect future returns

Yes. The new law beginning in 1998 allows you 120 days from the date you withdrew funds from your IRA to use them penalty-free for a first-time home purchase. If you do not use it, you can put the money back in your IRA without penalty. If you keep the money, but don't use it to buy a home, you will pay tax on it as well as a 10% penalty if you are less than 59½ years old.

179 **Last year I was able to make a $2,000 tax-deductible IRA contribution, but I only contributed $1,500. Can I make up the shortage this year by contributing $2,500—$2,000 for this year and $500 to make up the shortfall?**

No. There is no carryforward for a skipped year or for not contributing the maximum amount you could have. This goes for both traditional and the new Roth IRAs.

180 **Can I still contribute to my IRA after I reach my required beginning date at age 70½?**

New tax law will affect future returns

No, but there is one exception. Beginning in 1998 you can make nondeductible contributions after 70½ to the new Roth IRA (see *Question #170*).

181. How much can I contribute to my spouse's IRA if he or she does not work outside of the home?

Good news! Maximum spousal IRA contributions have been increased.

But first I should explain that a spousal IRA is an IRA plan set up for a spouse who has little or no compensation, formerly known as the "nonworking spouse." Under the old law, the contribution was limited to $250, but beginning in 1997, the limit has been increased to $2,000. The new limit is based on the total compensation of both spouses, so if one spouse earns at least $4,000, both spouses may make deductible IRA contributions of $2,000 each. To qualify, the couple must file a joint return.

'97 New tax law will affect 1997 returns

182. My husband is not eligible to make a deductible IRA contribution because he works for a company that has a pension plan. But the company I work for does not have a pension plan. Can I make a tax-deductible contribution to my IRA?

It depends which tax year you are asking about because the new tax law makes things increasingly easier for you beginning in 1998. So I have different answers for 1997 and 1998.

1997 tax year answer
It all depends on your Adjusted Gross Income (AGI). Even though your company does not have a plan, the fact that your husband's company has one triggers the IRA rules for deductibility. If you and your spouse's combined AGI exceeds $50,000, then you may not make a tax-deductible IRA contribution. If your combined AGI is less than $40,000, then you're under the income limit, and you may make a deductible IRA contribution (of up to $2,000, if you earn that much or more). Then, between $40,000 and $50,000 the availability of the IRA deduction phases out. For unmarried individuals, the phaseout range is AGI of $25,000 to $35,000.

If you still feel you would like to make an IRA contribution, you can always make a nondeductible contribution, but you must keep records of these contributions. You do this by filing Form 8606 on an annual basis to keep track of the amount of nondeductible contributions you have made to your IRA plan, so that when you take the money out, you'll know how much of each payment you'll have to pay tax on.

1998 and subsequent tax years answer

New tax law will affect future returns

With the new tax law, beginning in 1998, you are no longer considered an active participant in a pension plan just because your spouse is, so the usual income limitations apply only if you yourself have a retirement plan at work. The new tax law gradually increases the phaseout range for those with work-related pension plans to eventually double the 1997 amounts as follows:

Phaseout range

Year	Married-joint	Single or Head of household
1998	$50,000 - $60,000	$30,000 - $40,000
1999	$51,000 - $61,000	$31,000 - $41,000
2000	$52,000 - $62,000	$32,000 - $42,000
2001	$53,000 - $63,000	$33,000 - $43,000
2002	$54,000 - $64,000	$34,000 - $44,000
2003	$60,000 - $70,000	$40,000 - $50,000
2004	$65,000 - $75,000	$45,000 - $55,000
2005	$70,000 - $80,000	$50,000 - $60,000
2006	$75,000 - $85,000	$50,000 - $60,000
2007 and later	$80,000 - $100,000	$50,000 - $60,000

But—and there is always one more but when it comes to tax law—if your spouse has a pension plan at work, even this new level of availability phases out between combined AGI of $150,000 to $160,000. So, the bottom line is: starting in 1998, if you are not an active participant in a company plan but your spouse is, you can still make a tax-deductible $2,000 IRA contribution as long as your AGI does not exceed $150,000.

If neither you nor your spouse participate in a company retirement plan, you always could, and you still can, deduct your full IRA contribution regardless of your income.

183 Can I borrow from my 401(k) plan?

Yes, if the plan itself allows it, but there are limits. You may borrow the lesser of 50% of your 401(k) account or $50,000 without triggering a tax. Or, if you have less than $10,000, you can borrow all of it. The loan must be repaid in at least quarterly installments over no more than five years, unless it's for buying a principal residence. If you do not repay the loan within five years, or you miss a quarterly installment, it is treated as a taxable distribution and is subject to a 10% penalty if you are less than 59½ years old.

If you are fired or quit, the loan becomes a taxable distribution to you if the terms of your company's loan agreement are not satisfied. For example, if your plan agreement states that you must repay the loan within 60 days of termination of employment and you don't, the plan administrator will consider the loan to be a taxable distribution. In addition to the tax, you could be subject to a 10% penalty if you are under 59½ years old.

If you are self-employed, you cannot borrow from your plan.

184 **I am 52 years old, and because the large company I work for is downsizing, I have been laid off. I have accumulated over $200,000 in my company pension plan, which I may need if I cannot find new employment soon. I know about the 10% penalty for taking money out of a plan before age 59½, but is there any way to avoid it? Also, what should I do with my distribution if I do find work and want to move my old company's pension funds to my new employer's plan?**

Leaving with your pension
Downsizing, re-engineering, rightsizing, or whatever they are calling it this week, has hit many workers who are far from ready to retire. From the tax point of view, the important thing here is to know the rules and not lose your pension to tax traps. Also, there *are* exceptions to the general rules that let you tap your pension before its time.

First, the basics
The first thing to do is have your pension funds transferred directly from your company plan to a new IRA rollover account. This is called a trustee-to-trustee transfer and will bypass the 20% withholding tax provisions (see *Question #194* for more on this).

It is also important that you do not commingle your pension funds with existing IRA accounts. To avoid this pitfall you'll need to set up a new IRA rollover account. There is a big difference between regular IRA accounts and IRA rollover accounts. While the regular IRAs are the accounts to which you make annual contributions of up to $2,000, the IRA

Tax trap!

rollover account is created as a conduit for transferring qualified pension plan money to a new company's plan. If you mix regular and rollover IRA accounts, you will taint the new moneys and no longer be able to transfer them into a new employer's plan when, and if you get another job. Also, do not make additional IRA contributions to the rollover account. This will also taint the fund.

Early withdrawal options

As far as the 10% penalty for withdrawals before age 59½, there are several options. The first two are death and total disability, which are not worth it, so let's move on. Since you're 52 years old, you also do not qualify under the "separation from service" exception for employees who are at least age 55 upon discharge, retirement, or resignation (see ***Question #185***). Although tapping your nest egg should be the very last resort, you can take it free of the 10% penalty if you draw down each year as part of a series of what the tax law calls "substantially equal payments," i.e., by annuitizing over five years or until you reach age 59½, whichever is longer. The payout amount is determined by your life expectancy or the joint life expectancy of you and your beneficiary according to IRS actuarial tables. During the payout period the payment schedule cannot change, or the 10% penalty will be assessed retroactively to all amounts distributed before 59½ years old, and it will be as if you never qualified for the exception.

How should you do it? First decide how much you think you will need on an annual basis, then transfer enough to produce that amount into a separate IRA and draw from there. The rest of the money can continue to grow tax deferred—if you choose to annuitize, it doesn't mean you have to annuitize the entire IRA balance.

Other exceptions to the 10% penalty are as follows:
- *Distributions from qualified plans that are used to pay deductible medical expenses that exceed 7.5% of Adjusted Gross Income (whether or not you itemize)* Beginning in 1997, this medical expense exception also applies to early distributions (before 59½ years old) from regular IRAs.

- *You can also, beginning in 1997, make early withdrawals if you use them to pay for medical insurance for you and your family in the event you become unemployed and receive unemployment insurance for 12 consecu-*

New tax law will affect 1997 returns

tive weeks No distributions may be made later than 60 days after you become reemployed.

- *Beneficiaries who receive distributions from an IRA or pension are also exempt from the 10% penalty, regardless of their age, or the age of the deceased pension or IRA participant's age* Of course, all distributions from traditional IRAs are taxable.

Once you reach age 59½, you may withdraw as much or as little as you like from the account until you reach 70½ years of age (your required beginning date). When you reach 70½ years of age, you must withdraw certain minimum amounts each year, calculated by one of the three methods covered in *Question #191*.

185 I am older than 55, and have been laid off. Are there any special options to tap my retirement plan?

If you're age 55 or over and separated from service (laid off, fired, resigned, retired, etc.), you will not be hit with the 10% penalty for withdrawals from your corporation's qualified retirement plan before age 59½. This is a special exception to the 10% penalty, known as the "separation from service exception." It is not available for IRA distributions.

Good tax law

186 I have started my own new business and set it up as a corporation. I am the sole shareholder. I need start-up capital. Can I borrow from my IRA for this?

No. There are just certain things that you cannot do with your IRA moneys and this is one of them.

Things not to do with your IRA
Stocks, bonds, mutual funds, CDs, savings accounts, and U.S. Treasury bonds are all popular places to invest IRA moneys. Although the investment options may seem practically limitless, there are a few things you absolutely cannot do with your IRA funds. They are called "prohibited transactions," and carry severe penalties.

Prohibited transactions
Simply put, prohibited transactions for IRAs are investments or forms of self-dealing that would put the government at risk of losing its tax on the IRA.

IRS Publication 590 and the Internal Revenue Code define a prohibited transaction as "any improper use of your IRA account…by you or any disqualified person." A "disqualified person" is defined as a fiduciary, a member of your family, or any other entity such as a corporation, partnership, trust, or estate that is 50% or more controlled by you or your family members. For an IRA plan, you, the IRA owner, are a fiduciary, even though you're not the plan custodian. This is because you have discretion and control over the plan's investments.

The following types of transactions are specifically prohibited by the Internal Revenue Code:

- *Personally buying, selling, or leasing any property to or from your IRA* This is self-dealing and your IRA plan cannot engage in these transactions with you, even if the price is reasonable and fair. This includes setting up your own corporation and having it funded by your IRA plan, which would then buy stock in your new company.

- *Borrowing from or lending money to your IRA* You cannot borrow from your IRA or use or pledge it as collateral for a loan, even if the interest rate and other loan terms are fair. Any amount pledged as security for a loan will be treated as a taxable distribution.

- *Buying property for personal use with IRA funds*

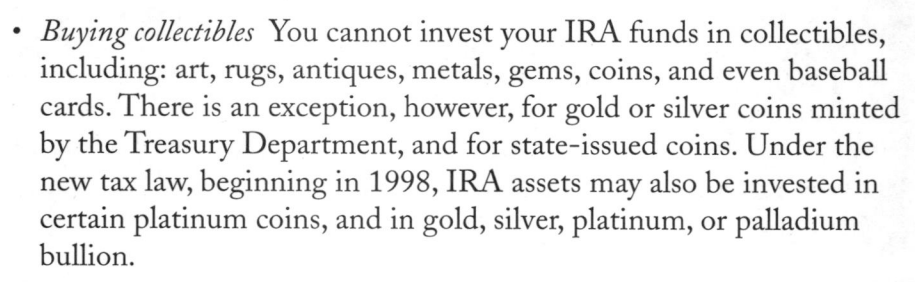

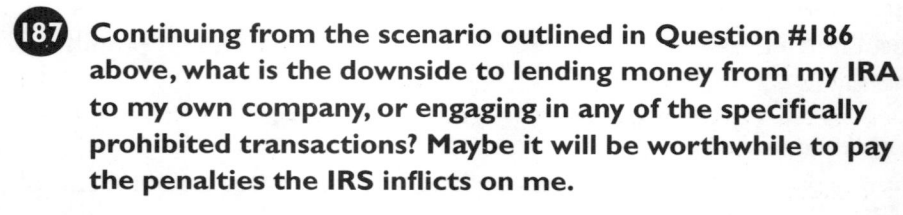

- *Buying collectibles* You cannot invest your IRA funds in collectibles, including: art, rugs, antiques, metals, gems, coins, and even baseball cards. There is an exception, however, for gold or silver coins minted by the Treasury Department, and for state-issued coins. Under the new tax law, beginning in 1998, IRA assets may also be invested in certain platinum coins, and in gold, silver, platinum, or palladium bullion.

- *Buying life insurance* You cannot use your IRA to buy life insurance.

187 **Continuing from the scenario outlined in Question #186 above, what is the downside to lending money from my IRA to my own company, or engaging in any of the specifically prohibited transactions? Maybe it will be worthwhile to pay the penalties the IRS inflicts on me.**

You don't really want to know. It is possibly the worst financial mistake you can make. The combination of penalties (if you're under 59½) and income taxes can quickly wipe out your only retirement plan and leave you with nothing when you may need it the most. Also, unless your business is the one in a thousand that will be an overnight success, you will have real financial problems when it comes to tax time and you have no money to pay the tax and penalties because your business ate it all up. The government places that excuse on an even keel with "the dog ate it."

What happens if there are prohibited transactions?

If you, the IRA owner, or your IRA beneficiary engage in a prohibited transaction, the IRA plan is disqualified retroactive to the first day of the year. The IRA is treated as if the entire account is taxable, retroactive to January 1 of the year of the prohibited transaction.

The distribution is taxable to the IRA owner and can be further subject to the 10% premature withdrawal penalty if the IRA owner is under 59½ years old as of the deemed date of the distribution, which is the first day of the year.

Example:
You're 55 years old and have an $125,000 IRA account at your bank. On September 30, 1998, you use $100,000 of it to buy a vacation condo as an IRA investment. This is a prohibited transaction, even if the home was bought at fair market value from an unrelated party. The entire $125,000 account will be disqualified—the IRS no longer considers it an IRS account—retroactive to January 1, 1998. The $125,000 will be a fully taxable distribution and will carry an additional 10% ($12,500 in this case) penalty, since you were under 59½ years old on January 1, 1998, the deemed date of the distribution. In addition, there are other costly excise taxes on prohibited transactions. So don't do it!

188 I am receiving a lump sum distribution from my company plan. What are my options?

You can either roll it over to your IRA or take a lump sum distribution if you qualify for favorable five or ten-year averaging. If you go the IRA rollover route, make sure to make a trustee-to-trustee transfer so that you don't get caught in the 20% tax trap (see **Question #194**). Also, remember to keep the funds in a separate IRA rollover account—with no funds from any other IRAs—in case you want to move it to a new employer's plan (see **Question #184**). Payments from a 403(b) or a Section 457 plan are not eligible for five or ten-year averaging, and Section 457 plans cannot be rolled over to an IRA. Section 457 plans are also not subject to the 10% early withdrawal penalty for distributions before age 59½ years old.

Five or ten-year averaging allows you to withdraw your lump sum and pay tax on it at a lower tax rate, since the IRS figures the rate as though you had withdrawn it over five or ten years. To qualify for either five or ten-year averaging you must have participated in a company retirement or Keogh plan for at least five years before your distribution, and the lump sum must be paid to you within one year of your leaving the company. You must also be at least 59½ years old at the time of the distribution. Beginning in the tax year 2000, the five-year option will be eliminated, leaving only ten-year averaging as an option; however, you must have been born before 1936 to qualify for ten-year averaging. Ten-year averaging will produce the lower tax if your distribution is less than $350,000 for 1997.

Another consideration is your need for cash. If you need the funds now, you can pay a lower tax with averaging and have unrestricted use of your money. If, on the other hand, you have other non-retirement funds to live on, I'd recommend that you use that money and roll your pension over to an IRA account to keep it growing tax-deferred for as long as possible.

189 I received my husband's retirement death benefit from his company. Is this taxable?

Yes, unless he died before August 20, 1996, in which case the first $5,000 would be excluded from income. The 1996 tax act repealed this tax exclusion. If you are eligible, then you may roll it over to a new spousal rollover IRA, thus deferring payment of tax.

190 I know that I do not have to take distributions until I am 70½. I am 62 now. Would it be wise to take distributions before I have to?

Should you draw from your IRA before you have to? That depends on a few factors. Everyone's situation is different, but here are some general guidelines:

If you need the money to live on, or you are in a lower tax bracket than you will be when you must start making distributions, it may be reasonable to draw down some of that money. Another viable strategy is to use what remains after you've paid income tax to reduce your estate, either through gifting or by leveraging it with life insurance. This may be advantageous because at death, life insurance proceeds may be exempt from both estate and income taxes (see *Question #214* for details).

Also, beginning in 1998, it might pay to convert your existing IRA to a new Roth IRA, which would allow you to make tax-free distributions after you retire (see *Questions #169 and #170* for more details). However, the amount that you convert to Roth would be taxable, so that the younger you are, the greater the benefit of conversion.

New tax law will affect future returns

But one rule is clear: you should not take from your IRA before you are required to if you intend simply to deposit what's left after tax into a CD or other investment in your own name. All that you've accomplished is to stop the tax-deferred build-up and replaced what's left with a taxable investment.

Tax trap!

191 **I am close to being 70½ years old, and the banks and brokerages where I have my IRA accounts are asking me to select the method for taking my required distributions. Which method should I select?**

The first thing to do is talk with a financial adviser who understands the tax laws and is familiar with your personal situation, including assets in the plan, other investments and assets, and family members.

This decision is important because it is irrevocable once elected, and has long-term effects on how quickly or slowly your IRA will be distributed and taxed. Here are the general rules you need to know:

No fooling!...April 1 is IRA election day!
If you turned 70½ in 1997, two of the most important financial decisions of your life must be made by April 1, 1998.

The decisions concern the distribution method and the selection of beneficiaries for your IRAs, 401(k)s, and other tax-deferred retirement plan moneys. Once made, the tax effect of beneficiary selection becomes permanent.

Hot tip!

The first step is to educate yourself and actively plan your retirement distributions before going to your bank or brokerage. Whatever you do, don't let them make the decisions for you. Beneficiary selection has a long-term impact on how much income and estate tax will eventually be paid on the retirement accounts. There are family considerations as well as estate and income tax issues that must be addressed when choosing distribution methods and beneficiaries.

The 70½ rules

Let's start with the general rule: you must begin drawing your retirement plan money by your required beginning date, which is April 1 of the year following the calendar year in which you turned 70½. If you turned 70½ in 1997, your required beginning date is April 1, 1998 and your second distribution must be taken by December 31, 1998. To avoid two distributions in a single year, which could land you in higher tax bracket, it may pay to take your first required distribution by December 31 of the prior year, or December 31, 1997, in this example.

There are three distribution options available, called the "recalculation method," the "term certain" or "once calculated" method, and the "hybrid method." The distribution method must be elected by the required beginning date for distributions, but I recommend that it be made as soon as possible—in other words, while you're still breathing.

It is important to remember that the purpose of this election is to define the minimum withdrawals from your retirement accounts, so that the government no longer has to postpone the gratification of receiving the income tax associated with this deferred income. You can always withdraw more than the minimum specified by the methods below.

Recalculation method

The recalculation method is the most widely used method because unless you specifically indicate otherwise, it becomes the elected method by default. Under the recalculation method, the annual minimum distribution amount is determined by the annually recalculated joint life expectancy of you and your spousal IRA beneficiary per IRS actuarial tables. (You cannot use the recalculation method for a non-spouse designated beneficiary.)

For example, if you turned 70½ years old in September 1997, you're required to take your first distribution by April 1, 1998, and a second by December 31, 1998. This is the rule, even if you're still working. Look up your joint (yours and your wife's) life expectancy in the IRS tables (available in IRS Publication 590), using the ages you attained on your birthdays in the year you turned 70½.

In this example, you would use ages 70 and 67 if you and your spouse turned 70 and 67 on your respective birthdays in 1997. The IRS table shows a joint life expectancy of exactly 22.0 years. You divide the balance of all your IRA accounts as of December 31, 1996, by 22 to obtain the required minimum distribution that must be made by April 1, 1998. The next year, your recalculated joint life expectancy would be 21.2 years according to the tables, and you would divide the balance of all your accounts as of December 31, 1997 by that number to determine the minimum payment.

The required minimum distribution may be withdrawn from a single account if you like, or from any combination of accounts. The following year, and each succeeding year, the joint life expectancy would be recalculated using the same method. However, if the account holder or beneficiary dies, the IRS actuarial tables dictate a shorter payout period with larger distributions which could mean higher income taxes. When both you and your beneficiary die, the account becomes part of your estate and may be subject to estate tax.

Required distributions can be deferred

Under the old law, minimum distributions from qualified plans and IRAs had to begin by the required beginning date, which was April 1 of the year after you turned 70½ years old. Under the new law, effective in 1997, if you are still working at 70½, you can delay your initial required distribution until April 1 of the year after the year you finally retire if your employer allows you take advantage of this rule.

Good tax law

Be careful here, as this deferral only applies to qualified plans. Your regular IRA accounts are not qualified plans, so you still must make a withdrawal from them by your required beginning date, even if you are still working. Missing the required IRA distribution means a 50% penalty on the amount you should have withdrawn but did not. Don't look to the

Tax trap!

IRS for sympathy if you blow this—you won't be excused because you thought the new law applied to all IRAs.

This new deferral is also not available to individuals who own 5% or more of a business that employs them.

Term certain method

The other, more favorable method is the term certain method, where instead of an annual recalculation, the life expectancy is calculated only once—for the initial distribution, which is based on the sum of money you have in your account, divided by the actuarially determined number of years left in your and your beneficiary's lives. In each succeeding year, the initial life expectancy is reduced by one year and the calculation is repeated using the new end-of-year balance. If you outlive the term calculated on the first year of distribution, then you will receive no further distributions.

For required payouts during your lifetime, there is a 10-year rule known as the Minimum Distribution Incidental Benefit rule (MDIB), which applies when you name a beneficiary other than your spouse who is more than 10 years younger than you, like a child or grandchild. Use the MDIB table in IRS publication 590, Appendix E. When the IRA owner dies, though, the child reverts back to his true life expectancy and can stretch the payments over that period, less the number of years the original IRA owner was taking distributions.

For example, assume you name your child as your IRA beneficiary by your required beginning date. Assume further that your child is 39 years old when you begin your required distributions. According to the IRS tables, his life expectancy at 39 years old is 43.5 years. While you're alive, you draw down based on the MDIB table. If you are 71, the factor is 25.3 years. If you die in five years, your child then reverts to his or her own original life expectancy (the 43.5 years) and will continue to draw down the IRA over the next 38.5 years, which is his or her original 43.5 year life expectancy less the five years already drawn by you. In the event of the death of the beneficiary prior to the last withdrawal, withdrawals continue at the same rate by whoever inherits the IRA.

If your beneficiary is your spouse, you must elect term certain by the required beginning date or lose it as an option. If you do not elect it, the bank or broker will probably give you recalculation by default.

There are advisers who prefer the recalculation method because if you use it, you will never draw out your last dime of IRA money. In contrast, with the term certain method the annual required distributions are slightly higher, and if you outlive your term, the account is empty.

I usually recommend the term certain method because of the flexibility it provides a family to stretch IRA payments after the death of the IRA owner or the beneficiary. For example, with term certain you can use a life expectancy of possibly 40 years or more by naming a child or grandchild and using his or her actual life expectancy after you die, parlaying the IRA funds through the magic of compound interest and the tax-deferred growth into a powerful financial legacy the likes of which your children and grandchildren may never have the opportunity to establish on their own.

Hybrid method
This method incorporates features of both the term certain and recalculation methods. It involves complex calculations that require the services of a specialist in retirement distribution planning.

Selection of your IRA beneficiary
Your designated beneficiary must be selected by your required beginning date (the April 1 date).

Selection of the beneficiary will determine for how long you can stretch your required IRA distributions, because the duration of the withdrawals is based on the joint life expectancy of you and your designated beneficiary. For example, if you're 70 and marry a 20 year-old, you will have a long life expectancy. However, this only works with a spouse: selection of a non-spouse beneficiary who is more than 10 years younger than you mandates use of the MDIB (10-year) table discussed above.

You may choose whoever you wish as your IRA beneficiary, even someone to whom you're not related. If your beneficiary is young, for example a grandchild, you might want to use a trust. But be careful here—you want to be sure to create an irrevocable trust, because for IRA purposes a revocable living trust has a zero life expectancy, thus ending tax deferral at the time of your death. Never name your estate as your IRA beneficiary, since it also has no life expectancy at the time of your death. Naming your estate as your IRA beneficiary may be the most costly tax mistake of all, because it can be taxed at rates in excess of 80% (yes…I said in excess of 80%!) or even higher when you factor in the ravaging effects of a combined estate and income tax, and, in some cases, a 50% excise tax, not to mention your own state's versions of these taxes.

Now that you know you should never name your estate as your IRA beneficiary, I'm sure that you never will—unless you already have, unknowingly. How? By failing to name anyone as your IRA beneficiary, your estate by default will become your beneficiary. So check your plan document to make sure you have named a beneficiary. Furthermore, it's wise to name a secondary beneficiary as well, in case you outlive your first beneficiary.

Hot tip!

192 All I want to know is how to take money out of my pension when I retire, but there are so many penalties. How do I go about this without hitting one of those mines?

The first thing to do is get professional advice, and I do not mean the bank clerk or the operator behind the 800 number for all the mutual fund companies giving "free" advice in this highly complex area. Mistakes on pension withdrawals are costly because they usually represent huge sums of money that took you a lifetime to earn. They have serious income tax consequences and long-term estate and financial planning tax traps, not to mention plenty of possible penalties.

Hot tip!

Unfortunately, very few qualified advisers really know all the rules. Even the "experts," including the bankers and brokers who call themselves "retirement plan specialists," often make mistakes.

Before you consult anyone, it's up to you to educate yourself in the particular area that concerns you most. This can be done by reading or attending seminars and, believe me, there is no shortage of seminars. But start by reading, and then you'll be able to pose good questions at the seminar you choose to attend. Seminars are usually free or at nominal cost, but do not judge them by the quality of the coffee and cake. It's content that matters here. Seminars give you an opportunity to meet your prospective advisers and judge for yourself. When you find someone you think you might be comfortable with, ask for a free follow-up consultation. At the consultation, don't be afraid to ask tough direct questions and for referrals of satisfied clients whose tax and pension situation is similar to your own.

Seminars help bring good advisers together with people that need them. If you're in the New York City area, you're welcome to sit in on our free seminars. Call 1-(516) 536-8282 for further information. End of pitch!

You can also ask friends or relatives for referrals, but never let friends or relatives be your advisers, especially those "expert" relatives with free advice! Nothing is free! You will just pay, and pay later, and when you're dead, your family will keep on paying.

193. Specifically, what are the "tax traps" or penalties I should know about related to distribution of my retirement funds?

The only thing worse than paying tax on your pension is losing it to IRS tax penalties because you don't know the rules. Since our government considers tax-deferred pension and retirement plans to be the single biggest tax break given to individuals and businesses, they want to make sure that you play by the rules. To accomplish this, they've backed the rules with stiff penalties.

Problems occur when you take your pension or IRA out too early or too late, or when you take out too little. Each situation carries penalties ranging from 10% to 50% of your pension withdrawals.

The tax code contains literally thousands of rules on penalties for improper distributions. Here are the ones you need to know, explained in English:

Too early
If you take out your money too early (before age 59½), there is a 10% penalty, but there are ways around it. (See *Question #184* and Appendix B for more information.)

Too late and/or too little
You must begin drawing your retirement plan money by April 1 of the year following the calendar year in which you turned 70½. If you do not draw your required minimum distributions, you will be hit with an incredible 50% penalty on the amount that you should have taken but did

not. For example, if the life expectancy tables show that you must take a distribution of $40,000 for 1997 and you only take out $10,000, you will pay a penalty of $15,000, which is half of the $30,000 in additional funds that you should have drawn.

15% excise tax repealed
The new tax law repeals the 15% excise tax both on excess distributions from and excess accumulations within retirement plans such as IRAs and other pensions. Prior to 1997, there was a 15% excise tax which applied when annual distributions from your pension or IRA were deemed by law to be too high. The 1996 tax legislation suspended the excise tax on distributions from IRAs and pensions from 1997 to 1999, and the new tax law enacted in 1997 act repeals it, as well as the excess accumulations tax which was levied at death on large retirement accounts. Both taxes were repealed, retroactively to December 31, 1996.

194 **I have recently retired and will start receiving my pension soon. I have been warned not to receive the money directly or I will be hit with what is called the "20% pension tax." I realize that I have to pay tax on this money as I draw it, but is there something else that I should be worried about? I am over 59½ years old, so there should be no penalty. Is the 20% tax an additional tax? Please explain this to me.**

You're right to be concerned, although technically this is not a tax. However, it can cause tax problems and penalties for the unwary.

The 20% tax trap
The "20% tax" you were warned about is not an additional tax, but it sure can be a trap if you're not careful. In 1992, Congress was afraid that too many people were spending their retirement money before they retired, so they came up with a new law to encourage rollovers of distributions to IRAs or to other qualified company retirement plans, and to discourage taking the distributions as income and spending the money.

In its haste, Congress goofed, and what resulted has become a pension and retirement nightmare. Since January 1, 1993, retirement plan distributions that are eligible for rollovers are subject to a 20% withholding tax on the distribution, unless the distribution is rolled over in a trustee-to-trustee transfer. A trustee-to-trustee transfer means that the retirement check goes directly from your company pension plan to your IRA rollover account or to your new employer's plan. If it doesn't, the pension check will be reduced by the 20% withholding tax and could be subject to additional income taxes and penalties.

For example, say in January, 1998 you retire and are entitled to a lump sum pension distribution of $100,000. Under the old rules, you could have had the check made out to you for $100,000, and you had 60 days to decide whether to roll it over to an IRA rollover account or take it as income and pay the tax. Under the new law, if you want the check made out to you personally, you will only receive $80,000, since it will be subject to the mandatory 20% withholding of $20,000. You can still decide to roll over the money within the 60 days, but you now only have $80,000 to roll over. The $20,000 shortfall will have to be made up with other funds. If it is not, it will be treated as a taxable distribution and will be subject to income tax, as well as to a 10% premature distribution penalty of $2,000 if you're less than 59½ years old. If you're older than 59½ years, you don't have to worry about the 10% penalty.

The way to prevent this tax trap is to have the company pension plan send the check directly to your IRA rollover account in full. But watch out: some companies still have computer systems that automatically make the check out to you instead of allowing for trustee-to-trustee transfers. It's up to you to bring this to their attention and ask them not to.

Hot tip!

195 Who pays the income tax on an inherited IRA?

The person who inherits it (the IRA beneficiary). The income tax is paid on the annual amount(s) withdrawn at the beneficiary's own tax rates. If you're the beneficiary of an IRA or pension, you may be entitled to a big tax deduction that you can use to offset the income tax on the inherited IRA account. It's called the estate tax deduction. (See *Question #196* below for details.)

196 I am the beneficiary of an IRA that I inherited from my father. I know that I have to pay tax on distributions I take from this IRA account, but are there any other tax breaks I might be missing?

Yes. Possibly big ones. If your father's estate was a taxable estate—meaning that federal estate tax was paid and the IRA was included in the estate—you are now, as the beneficiary of this IRA, entitled to take an

Hot tip!

income tax deduction for the amount of the federal estate tax paid on the IRA. The purpose of this income tax deduction is to make sure that the same item, in this case, the IRA, does not get hit with both full estate tax and full income tax. This is called Income in Respect of a Decedent (IRD). Unfortunately, beneficiaries often pay this tax unnecessarily, because they don't know about this deduction.

For example, assume you inherited a $100,000 IRA account that was included in your father's estate. Assume further that the federal estate tax paid on the IRA was $40,000. If you, as the beneficiary, withdraw the entire $100,000 in one tax year, you might pay income tax on the full amount at your own income tax bracket. But now, since you bought this book, you realize that you're entitled to a $40,000 deduction for the tax previously paid. This is an itemized deduction which is not subject to the 2% limitation. It's called the estate tax deduction.

197 What are Medical Savings Accounts?

Medical Savings Accounts (MSAs) have arrived. The 1996 Health Reform Bill gives a limited number of small business employees and self-employed individuals an opportunity to establish MSAs, effective January 1, 1997. A small business for purposes of this provision is one with 50 or fewer employees.

MSAs are tax-deferred investment accounts used to store money which may someday be needed to pay medical bills. You must, however, have a high-deductible or catastrophic medical policy. The rationale is that you can carry a relatively inexpensive health insurance policy with a high deductible, while the money saved on premiums grows tax-deferred in your MSA until needed to pay medical expenses not covered by the policies.

How MSAs work

MSAs are set up either through insurance companies or other institutions (banks, brokers, etc.). They are similar to IRAs, except for the coupling with high-deductible health insurance policies. The contributions to MSAs are tax-deductible and the money in the account grows, tax-deferred.

Medical bills of up to $3,000 per year for single individuals and $5,500 for families can be paid from your MSA. The funds may be used to cover your medical policy's deductible and to meet other expenses that are not covered by your health insurance policy, such as eyeglasses and dental care. You may also pay your insurance co-payments out of an MSA. Any money left over in the MSA at the end of the year stays in the account and continues to grow, tax-deferred. If you withdraw money from the MSA for non-medical purposes, however, you will be subject to a 15% penalty plus regular income tax before age 65. Those 65 or older still pay the income tax, but no penalty.

MSA contribution limits

The amount you may contribute to your MSA is limited to 65% of the deductible for individual policies or 75% of the deductible for family policies. Either you or your employer, but not both, may contribute during any one year. As mentioned above, you must have a high-deductible medical policy, meaning deductibles from $1,500 to $2,250 for individuals and from $3,000 to $4,500 for families. An individual with a policy deductible of $2,000 can therefore contribute $1,300 (65% of $2,000). If she or he has a family and a deductible of $3,000, an annual contribution of $2,250 (75% of $3,000) would be allowed.

More MSA provisions

Like an IRA, you have until the April 15 tax return due date to make tax-deductible contributions to your MSA for the previous year. At death, any balance remaining in your MSA is included as income to your estate or your MSA beneficiary, but qualifies for the marital deduction if your spouse is your MSA beneficiary. Your spouse, if the designated beneficiary, may continue to use the MSA as his or her own after your death.

The jury is out...

MSAs are currently a pilot program that calls for 750,000 policies to be purchased during the four-year test period of 1997 to 2000. So far, through September 1997, there are plenty left—the MSAs have been far from gobbled up as Congress thought they would be.

MSAs are a gamble. If you stay healthy for the long haul you will be able to save thousands of dollars in premiums and grow those savings tax-deferred. MSAs are the newest experiment in helping people pay for their health care. We'll have to see how they work out...

198 What is a "SIMPLE" retirement plan?

Under the Small Business Job Protection Act of 1996, "SIMPLE "—an acronym for "Savings Incentive Match Plan for Employees" Retirement Plans replaced SARSEP, which stood for Salary Reduction Employee Pensions.

"SIMPLE" retirement plans
SIMPLE is a new plan available for small companies (with 100 employees or less) who have no other qualified plan. Under the SIMPLE plan, employees can make elective contributions to a SIMPLE 401 (k) or IRA account rather than a company pension plan. The employer can match the contributions and also get a tax deduction for those amounts contributed.

With the new SIMPLE plans, employees may contribute up to $6,000 per year, with the exact amount based on a percentage (up to 100%) of the employee's compensation. The $6,000 per year limit is indexed for inflation and will go up in $500 increments. To be eligible, employees must earn at least $5,000 per year. Employers must match employees' elective contributions (up to 3% of annual compensation) or under special rules (more rules!) may contribute as little as 1%.

But leave it to the government to make SIMPLE very complicated. Congress has come up with yet another penalty in this complicated IRA and pension area. This one is a 25% early withdrawal penalty. (As if 10% wasn't enough!) The 25% early withdrawal penalty applies when employees have to withdraw their contributions from the SIMPLE IRA within the first two years from the date they started the account. All this is an effort to keep it SIMPLE!

Existing SARSEP's are grandfathered, which means that if they were in effect before January 1, 1997, they can continue and can receive contributions under the old rules. If you already have a SARSEP and hired new employees after December 31, 1996, and those employees want to participate in the SARSEP, they may, under the grandfather clause.

SIMPLE plans became effective January 1,1997.

Section 13
Your Questions About Your Social Security Benefits and Taxes

Just remember, when you're over the hill, you begin to pick up speed.
   Charles Schulz

Until a few years ago, the fact that you were receiving Social Security benefits really had nothing to do with your taxes. Boy, have times changed! Now I find myself devoting many hours to the many tax decisions and calculations involving Social Security and my clients. Up to 85% of your benefits can now be taxed, and if you're eligible for benefits and continue to work, you could forfeit some or all of your Social Security if you're less than 70 years old. Recipients now wonder whether it even pays to work. Let's find out…

199 I'm 68 years old and receiving Social Security. I'm still working, and would like to continue to work, but it seems that I'm giving back more than I'm keeping. Does it pay to for me to keep working?

If you're 62 to 69 years old and are receiving Social Security benefits while you're still working, you may find that it just doesn't pay to work. However, if you're 70 or older, you may earn as much as you like without losing your Social Security.

Earnings limits for those aged 62 to 64
Workers who are 62 to 64 years old will lose $1 of Social Security benefits for every $2 earned over the 1997 threshold amount of $8,640.

Earnings limits increase for those aged 65 to 69
Beginning in 1997, individuals 65 to 69 years of age will be able to earn more in each passing year before their Social Security benefits are affected. If you're 65 to 69 years old, you will lose $1 of benefits for every $3 over a limit which increases annually as follows:

1997	$13,500	2000	$17,000
1998	$14,500	2001	$25,000
1999	$15,500	2002	$30,000

Really stupid tax law

Example:

To see how quickly your benefits erode, let's look at a simplified example: Let's say you're 62 and still working. Your wages will be subject to a FICA tax of 6.2% and to a Medicare tax of 1.45%, for a total of 7.65%. Add this 7.65% to a 50% loss of benefits and you're up to a 57.65% effective tax rate on your wages over $8,640, and that's before calculating the income tax you'll pay on these wages.

Income tax payments will further erode your hard-earned wages. If, for example, you're in a tax bracket with a 33% maximum tax rate (28% federal tax and 5% estimated state tax), your effective tax rate goes over 90% on excess earnings.

Really stupid tax law

Don't forget the tax on benefits

If your income exceeds certain levels, your Social Security benefits may become taxable as income. If you're 62 to 69 years old and want to work, then you may have your economic incentive to get up at 7 A.M. every morning eroded even further. There is no age exclusion from this provision. (See *Question #203* for more information.)

200 **I am 62 and still working. Should I elect to receive my Social Security benefits now or wait until age 65?**

It might be wise to elect not to receive benefits until you reach 65 years of age. If you elect to receive Social Security now, you will receive only 80% of the benefits you'll receive if you wait until age 65. The 80% amount stays for life (other than regular cost-of-living adjustments) and does not rise to 100% when you reach 65. If you're going to lose some or all of your Social Security because you work and earn too much (see *Question #199*), then it certainly does not pay to take it at 62 and only receive 80% for life.

When you hit 70 years old, there is no longer a Social Security penalty for working. However, up to 85% of your benefits may still be subject to tax, depending on your income (see *Question #203*). There is no age exemption from this rule.

Hot tip!

201 **If I am under 70 and continue to work, even though my wages are causing me to forfeit my benefits, will I receive anything back from Social Security for continuing to work?**

Yes, crumbs that will one day enable you to see a movie…alone.

Does it pay to continue working?

The advisers at most Social Security offices will tell you that it pays to work for those microscopic benefits you will receive…someday. If you've heard that line, as I'm sure many have, what they are referring to is the fact that you can recoup a small portion of Social Security benefits that you lost due to the earnings limits. It's called "Delayed Retirement Credits." If, at 65 years of age, your earnings were so high that under the "$1 of lost benefits for every $3 earned rule," you received no check at all, you will receive an additional benefit of 0.55% for each month that you did not receive a Social Security check. In real numbers, however, this comes out to about five dollars a month for a person whose full monthly benefit would otherwise have been $1,000 a month.

Continued earnings after age 62 or 65 can also increase your monthly benefit, independent of the rule invoked above, since the Social Security you receive is based on a percentage of your earnings averaged over most of your working lifetime.

202 **I am turning 70 this year and am looking forward to working more and earning more income, now that I no will longer have to forfeit benefits for earning over the limits. Exactly when am I eligible to do this?**

At age 70 you can work and earn as much as you like with no loss of benefits. When do you actually turn 70 for Social Security purposes? For the earnings limit test, it's on the first day of the month that includes your 70th birthday.

For example, if your 70th birthday is April 23, 1998, you're considered to be 70 years old as of April 1, 1998, and you can thereafter earn as much as you like without any loss of benefits. If you have earnings in the year you turn 70, Social Security will need to know exactly when (by month) they were earned. They will ask you to fill out an Annual Report of Earnings (Social Security Form SSA-777-SM), which will be due by the following April 15.

203. We are senior citizens who would like to get married. We are each receiving our own Social Security benefits. How would our marriage affect taxation of benefits?

You're not going to like this, because you may get hit big time with the IRS rules which can make your Social Security benefits as much as 85% taxable.

Taxation of Social Security benefits

Social Security benefits *can* be taxed. Yes, your hard-earned government pension, extracted from the wages you've been paying taxes on your whole working life, can become taxable—if you have enough income from other sources. And if that's not enough, if you bought municipal bonds to avoid federal income tax, the income from them counts toward figuring how much tax you owe on your Social Security!

Really stupid tax law

How much of your benefits is taxable depends on a special calculation of what I'll call "provisional income." Provisional income is calculated by adding the following:

- *50% of Social Security benefits*
- *"Tax-exempt" income, such as municipal bond interest*
- *Certain foreign-earned and otherwise excludable income*
- *Regular income, such as pensions, taxable interest, dividends, and wages*

If you're single and provisional income is $25,000 to $34,000 ($32,000 to $44,000 for married couples), up to 50% of your benefits may be subject to tax. If you're single with more than $34,000 in provisional income ($44,000 for married couples), you may find that up to 85% of your benefits are subject to tax.

Bad tax law

What all this means is that two individuals who remain single will be way ahead of where they would be if they had married, since they can earn up to $50,000 ($25,000 multiplied by 2 equals $50,000) before benefits start being taxable. On the other hand, for married folks, benefits become taxable as provisional income rises above $32,000. Result: the two single individuals can earn an additional $18,000 before this nefarious grab by the IRS kicks in.

Taxation of Social Security benefits may lead to another tax trap, since it can raise your income to a point where it causes your IRA to be nondeductible if one of the spouses is an active participant in a company pension plan.

204. Should I invest in municipal bonds to keep my income under the threshold amount that will trigger taxation of my Social Security benefits?

No. Although tax-exempt interest is not taxable, it is included in the base amount of income used to determine how much of your Social Security will be taxed. One-half of Social Security benefits received is also added to this amount (see *Question #203* above for more on this issue).

Bad tax law

205. I am receiving Social Security benefits which are currently 85% taxable (see Question #203). This money is being used almost entirely to pay my medical expenses. Can I use my medical expenses as a deduction to reduce or eliminate taxation of my Social Security?

Although this sounds fair to me, the answer is, "not directly." An expense cannot be used to directly reduce the amount of Social Security that will be taxable. However, if medical expenses are high enough to be deductible, which means they exceed 7.5% of your Adjusted Gross Income, they can indirectly reduce the amount of tax that is paid on Social Security by reducing or eliminating your total income, which of course, includes the 85% of Social Security benefits.

206. Gosh darn it, is there anything I can do about lowering the tax on my Social Security?

Yes. Lower your income. There are no other ways to escape the tax on Social Security. As I mentioned in the answer to *Question #203*, even investing in tax-free municipal bonds will not lower that tax.

Section 14
Your Estate Planning and Taxes

There's no reason to be the richest man in the cemetery. You can't do any business from there.
   Colonel Harlan Sanders

A pot of gold at the end of the rainbow. That's what your government thinks of your estate. You, on the other hand, have to plan to make sure the assets you've accumulated over a lifetime of working and saving go where you want them to go. Yet, the sad fact is, most people do nothing about estate planning.

The federal estate tax begins at 37% and moves up quickly to 55%. Even though a married couple with assets under $1.2 million in 1997 should pay no estate tax, many do because they never bothered with estate planning. I like to tell couples that if they have assets of $1.2 million or less in 1997, paying estate tax is voluntary.

The larger the estate, the more likely it is that the IRS will audit your estate return. Why? Because it's their last chance to get you. But this is an area where you can do something that will make a difference. I'll tell you how...

207 What is all this about estate planning? Isn't estate planning only for the rich?

Not only isn't this true, but the less you have, the more you should plan to protect it. Your estate may not get the media attention the Jacqueline Onassis estate auction did, but that doesn't mean that you can't benefit from good planning.

Hot tip!

Estate planning isn't only about saving estate taxes. People think, "If I have a small estate, I won't owe any estate taxes, so I don't need estate planning." Wrong!

A final common misconception is that estate planning simply means making a will. Although saving estate taxes and drawing up a will are part of a good estate plan, there are other issues to consider, regardless of your wealth...or the lack of it. Let me explain:

Estate planning for young families

Estate planning is essential for young families in order to protect their minor children in case of a tragedy resulting in the death of both parents. Parents should choose a guardian for minor children and provide direction on how the children are to be raised. And they need to pick a custodian to manage life insurance money or other funds on behalf of the children.

Estate planning also involves making health care decisions. There may come a time when disability, incapacity, or incompetence limits or severely impacts your decision-making capabilities. Appoint someone to make medical and financial decisions for you in the event you become unable to make them for yourself. A health care proxy and a properly drawn durable power of attorney can help accomplish this. A living trust may be the preferable choice for managing assets during disability or passing them on at death (see **Question #217**).

Making decisions

The key to estate planning is making decisions before they are made for you. Although decision-making holds many people back from completing their estate plan (especially naming guardians for children), the choices will be made anyway at some point by someone. Your best move is to make those tough decisions now. It really is your responsibility, and if you don't fulfill it, some state-appointed guardian will. Your worst decision is likely to be better than someone else's best decision.

Estate planning: a gift to the survivors

Estate planning is so much more than simply dividing up your property. The best gift you can give your family is direction and a plan. Let them know your wishes. This will avoid confusion, costly litigation, and a will contest later on. It will also promote family unity after death.

208 Is my estate big enough to worry about estate planning?

Your estate is larger than you think

The fact is, most people grossly underestimate the size of their estate, because they do not figure in the value of a home, life insurance, a family business, pensions, IRAs, and joint accounts, not to mention that house in the country or the Florida condo. When you add it all up, you may very well have an estate that exceeds the $600,000 exempt from IRS taxation. Some states, however, have a lower limit than the federal $600,000, while others, Florida, for example, have effectively no estate tax.

209 What is the estate tax exemption?

This is actually both an estate and gift tax exemption and it is the amount that a person can transfer during life as a gift or pass on at death in their estate free of federal gift and estate taxes. For 1997, the federal gift and estate tax exemption is $600,000, but the new tax law changes that.

Estate tax changes

Beginning in 1998, the federal gift and estate tax exemption will gradually increase, as indicated below, to $1 million by 2006.

Year	Exemption
1998	$625,000
1999	$650,000
2000	$675,000
2001	$675,000
2002	$700,000
2003	$700,000
2004	$850,000
2005	$950,000
2006	$1,000,000

New tax law will affect future returns

210 What is probate?

Probate is a judicial process by which a will is validated and by which the wishes expressed in the will are carried out. During this process, a combination of court costs, legal fees, and other expenses are incurred. But probate itself is not, as many believe, a tax. Rather, the probate court is the forum where the validation of the will is carried out.

Probate has good points and bad points. On the one hand, the probate process serves to protect the rights and wishes of the deceased. On the other hand, probate can be time consuming and costly, often depending on the state in which it is being carried out. California and Florida are examples of states in which probate is painful, and thus many Californians and Floridians have set up living trusts to avoid probate. **Probate can also be a problem if the will is contested, or if property ownership** issues need to be resolved. Keep in mind that probate is also a public process—privacy is not protected.

The probate process covers property that is directed by your will. For example, if you state in your will, "I leave my house to my daughter," that house will go through probate to make sure it goes to your daughter, the named beneficiary in the will.

However, there are certain items that pass outside the will and thus are not probate property. You do not have to take special steps to avoid probate on such assets.

Non-probatable property (passes outside the will)
- *Jointly owned property with right of survivorship*
- *Life insurance with a named beneficiary*
- *Pensions, IRAs, and Keoghs with designated beneficiaries*
- *Property owned by a revocable "living" trust*

It is important to remember that estate tax will be assessed on some assets which are non-probate—for example, pensions, IRA's, Keoghs, and property placed in a revocable living trust. On the other hand, property may be subject to probate but not to estate tax, for example, if one's estate is valued below the 1997 $600,000 federal exemption in a state which also has an exemption of that magnitude or greater.

211) We planned our estate about ten years ago. How often and when should it be updated?

Estate plans are not permanent. They should change or be updated as your family changes. Every time there is a birth, death, marriage, divorce, or a change in any of the other facts that you relied upon to plan your estate, plans should be updated. For example, your only daughter marries a bum…you may want to make some changes.

Your health and the health of your family members are also considerations. If you have named an executor or trustee who is now mentally incapacitated or unable to serve, you should make a change. You should change your documents when children are able to take on more responsibility, or when they may want to take on less responsibility because of their own problems.

For couples who have named guardians for their young children, plans may have to be amended if the guardians they have chosen are no longer suitable, or if they have moved across the country and it is no longer practical to have them serve as guardians.

Estate plans must take into account changes in tax law. However, properly drafted wills and trusts often anticipate tax law changes and may not require modification with each new move that Congress makes. One exception was the 1993 tax act that retroactively raised estate taxes. Yes, they actually raised taxes on people who were already dead. But, you know, they received no complaints from those people! Those guys in Congress are pretty smart, hey?

212 Can I beat Uncle Sam out of an estate tax by moving to another country and renouncing my U.S. citizenship?

No. If you try this to avoid taxes, you'll have to pay a pretty steep exit tax, which it turns out amounts to paying your estate tax before you move abroad…just in case you happen to forget about it later. Not only will you be subject to these hefty up-front estate taxes, but there are also new information and reporting requirements that stretch for ten years after you relinquish your citizenship. The new expatriation provisions apply to individuals who lose or renounce U.S. citizenship or U.S. residency after February 5, 1995.

My advice is to stay here and die in the good old USA…but do some good estate planning first.

213 Is my life insurance included in my estate?

Probably, depending on how it is owned. If you, the insured, own the policy, as most people do, the life insurance proceeds will be included in your taxable estate and could trigger a whopping estate tax. If the policy is for a large amount of money, it could cause an estate tax on what might have been a nontaxable estate. Or it could bump your estate up into a higher tax bracket.

This tax vulnerability can be avoided if your insurance is kept out of the estate.

Hot tip!

214. How can I arrange to keep my life insurance benefits out of my estate?

Life insurance proceeds are tax-free for income tax to the beneficiaries named in the policy, but they are not exempt from estate tax if you own the policy yourself. Therefore, people should generally not own their own life insurance policy. It should either be owned outright by the beneficiaries or be placed in an irrevocable trust. A good insurance professional will educate you on this up front, and help you plan to keep insurance out of your estate.

Hot tip!

Let me give you the scoop on how to do it. Look at your current insurance policies to see if they can be transferred out of your name, either to an irrevocable trust or directly to the beneficiaries. Watch out for gift taxes here. If you want to transfer your policies out of your name to a trust or beneficiary, you first have to see what the policy is worth. Generally, this is the cash surrender value. You must also deduct any outstanding loans on the policy. This "net" value is the true amount you're transferring and will be the amount of the gift. If this amount exceeds the annual $10,000 or $20,000 gift limits, then there may be a gift tax problem, or you could wind up using some of your 1997 estate and gift tax $600,000 exemption. Losing some of the exemption may still be worth it, if the amount of insurance benefits you're removing from your estate is large enough.

The three-year rule

If you wish to transfer an existing policy to keep it out of your estate, you should be aware that if you die within three years of the date of the transfer, the insurance money will go back into your estate for purposes of calculating the estate tax due. But if you do not transfer it, it will end up in your estate anyway, so you really have nothing to lose. There is no three-year rule with new policies; the rule only applies to existing policies that are transferred.

215 What happens if my heirs do not have the money to pay estate taxes? Although my estate appears large, there is not much cash, and most of the estate assets are tied up in real estate, IRA accounts, and a family business.

The IRS does not care. They want their money, in cash, within nine months of the date of death. You will have to start selling things off or tap those IRA accounts, which is probably the worst possible tax move.

Paying estate taxes from tax-deferred accounts, like IRA's, pensions, or annuities, starts a vicious cycle of taxation that can quickly ravage these assets at the most excessive total tax rates, reaching levels of outright confiscation in some cases.

Tax trap!

The solution is to plan for estate liquidity by having available life insurance or funds which are not in tax-deferred accounts.

Plan ahead
Plan ahead for estate liquidity. Look now for possible sources of money to pay estate taxes. Look at life insurance for maximum leverage. Also, look at second-to-die insurance policies (sometimes called survivor or two-life policies) to pay estate taxes. These policies pay off at the death of the second spouse, which is when most people need the money to pay estate taxes.

Hot tip!

New family business and farm tax break
Beginning in 1998, the first $1.3 million of value of a family farm or business will be exempt from federal estate tax. (Beware: this $1.3 million is not in addition to the regular 1997 $600,000 estate tax exemption, so if you own a business, your maximum total exemption is $1.3 million.) The value of the business must exceed 50% of the decedent's estate to qualify, and the business generally must be retained by the family for at least ten years. There are numerous conditions and complications attached to this tax break. It doesn't matter how the business is owned, that is, whether it's a corporation, partnership, limited liability company, or self-employed business. But the exemption cannot be used for public companies, and for public companies that change back to private ownership, there's a three year look-back rule. The 50% test may be harder to meet than it appears because certain assets of the business don't count towards the estate. These include assets like excess cash (cash that the govern-

New tax law will affect future returns

Good tax law

ment feels is in excess of that required to run the business) and passive assets—marketable securities, or those assets that produced dividends, interest, rent income, royalties, or annuities. To get this family tax break, you must fulfill the following conditions:

- *The decedent must be a U.S. citizen or a resident at the time of death*

- *The family business must be bequeathed to qualified heirs* A "qualified heir" may be a family member or "key-man employee." A key-man employee is a worker who has been employed for at least ten years prior to the date of the owner's death.

- *The business must have been owned and materially operated as a family business for at least five of the eight years preceding death*

There are also penalties which may apply if certain events, called "recapture provisions," occur following the death of the owner. When these kick in, the heirs become personally liable for repaying to the government the tax benefits they have received. The recapture events are as follows:

- *A qualified heir ceases to materially participate in the business*

- *A qualified heir disposes of any portion of his or her interest (other than to a member of the qualified heir's family)*

- *A qualified heir loses U.S. citizenship*

- *The business moves out of the U.S.*

Low interest installment payments for family businesses and farms

There are payment arrangements that the IRS will make with you to avoid your having to sell off a family business or farm which had been owned by a decedent. Under Section 6166 of the tax code, you can pay the estate tax in installments over 14 years at a very favorable 4% interest rate. Beginning in 1998, this rate drops even further, to 2%, but the interest is no longer deductible, as was the previous 4% interest. Those who were using this installment payment option before the law change may make a one-time election to use the lower interest rate (thus giving up their interest deduction). But, as with anything that sounds this good, there are conditions, and one of them is that the family keep the business or farm going. If it's sold within the payment period, the deal is off and the tax is due.

To qualify for this tax break, the value of the business or farm must be more than 35% of the total estate, and there is a $1 million cap on the value of the business or farm upon which estate tax can be deferred. This cap is high enough to help many small and family-owned businesses and farms avoid liquidation to pay estate taxes.

216 What is a revocable "living" trust?

A trust of any kind is an agreement in writing between the one creating the trust (the grantor or trustor) and the one responsible for carrying out the terms or obligations of the trust (the trustee). A trust also has one or more beneficiaries who are the people for whom the trust was set up to ultimately benefit. Each state has its own laws on legal and technical structuring of trusts, but generally, a trust can be as rigid or liberal as the grantor wishes. A trust can also be revocable (changeable or reversible) or irrevocable (not changeable, etched in stone, permanent).

A trust can be a living (or "inter-vivos") trust or a testamentary trust. A living trust is created during the life of the grantor. A testamentary trust is created at death under the terms of a will.

You can create a trust for virtually any lawful purpose. Trusts are sometimes created to keep one's wishes in effect after death. Using trusts, you can, as it has been aptly noted, "rule from the grave."

217 What are the advantages of a revocable living trust?

If you're concerned about the time delays and expense of probate, a living trust may be for you, since assets titled in the name of the living trust avoid probate. If you have a substantial estate, the living trust is a popular vehicle to avoid the potentially lengthy process and higher cost of probate. However, property in a revocable living trust is still subject to estate tax, since it is included in your estate.

A living trust can also be a big benefit to people who own property in two or more states, because it will avoid what is known as "ancillary probate," which is the process of probating out-of-state property in a number of different states.

Hot tip!

Living trusts are ideal for unmarried couples who want to keep their affairs and wishes private, and to protect against possible challenges to their wills, especially by family members who may not have approved of the relationship. A living trust maintains privacy—unlike a will, it is not a matter of public record.

Property placed into a living trust can also be continuously managed during disability and incompetence without having to have a court appoint a guardian to manage your affairs. A living trust can be set up by appointing a trustee of your choice who can, in the event of your mental incapacitation, step in to manage property and financial affairs without state or bureaucratic interference.

If you're considering using a living trust, make sure the trust document is prepared by an attorney who specializes in this area. You may also need to seek tax advice on the best ways to fund the trust in order to take advantage of the 1997 $600,000 estate tax exemptions in your, and if you're married or living together, your spouse's or partner's estate.

218 Do you need an attorney to prepare a revocable living trust?

Yes! Or don't bother at all.

This is a complicated area and you should be guided by professionals. Each trust, depending on how it is set up, may be subject to different estate, gift, and income tax treatment. Knowing how to use trusts to accomplish family goals regarding the preservation and disposition of assets, and at the same time, achieving maximum estate, gift, and income tax benefits, is a key to estate planning. Estate planning may appear expensive, often running $5,000 and up in tax and legal fees, but if done correctly by competent professionals (your CPA and attorney), it can save you more than a hundred times those fees in estate tax savings, not to mention perpetuating your family's wealth for generations. Never underestimate the value of good, creative estate planning guided by professionals. It may be the single best investment you ever make!

219 Which saves more in estate taxes, a will or a living trust?

Neither a will nor a living trust are universal cure-alls, and neither one magically saves any more in estate taxes than the other. A living trust is funded while you're alive, thus giving you input on how your assets will be divided. On the other hand, if trusts are set up at death by a will, you'll have to hope they are properly funded at that time.

A living trust is not a substitute for a will. It is a management vehicle designed to be effective both during life and after death, with little or no court intervention. Younger folks may decide to have both a living trust (to arrange for disposition of their assets), and a will (to name guardians for minor children, something you cannot do with a trust).

Because one of the biggest benefits of a living trust is that it avoids probate, it has no effect on property which is already exempt from probate. Jointly owned property, pensions, IRA's, and life insurance are examples of non-probate property.

Property in the revocable trust is included in, and can be taxed as part of your estate. If you want to remove property from your estate, you must create an irrevocable trust.

220 If I have a revocable living trust, do I have to file a separate tax return each year for the trust?

No. This trust is what the IRS calls a "grantor trust," which means that all income during your life flows back to you, the grantor (the one who set up and funded the trust). You report the income on your regular personal tax return just as you always did. You also do not need a separate tax identification number for the trust until you die. At death the trust becomes irrevocable and is required to start filing its own trust tax return (Form 1041).

221 I have a living trust and would like to make gifts from my living trust to my children. Can I do this without tax problems?

Yes. The old law was unclear on this, and tax court rulings went both ways on this issue. But the new tax law enacted in 1997 resolved this issue in favor of taxpayers. Yea!

Good tax law

Living trust tax relief
Gifts made from living trusts within three years before death may no longer be brought back into the estate and taxed as mandated by previous tax law. Effective for decedents whose deaths occurred after August 5, 1997, gifts from revocable trusts will be treated for tax purposes as if made directly by the grantor (the one who set up the trust). In the past, people with assets in living trusts were warned not to make the $10,000/

New tax law will affect 1997 returns

$20,000 annual exclusion gifts directly from their revocable living trusts because of possible estate tax inclusion if they died within three years of the gift. The new law eliminates this problem.

222. I've heard living trusts are not public and can be used to maintain privacy. Does this mean that assets in a living trust are also protected from the IRS?

No. Assets in a living trust are part of your estate. The IRS can, and often does, look into assets in your living trust that are part of your estate, but the IRS is not allowed to make your information public.

Think about it. If there were a place where you could put assets that would be legally concealed from the IRS, don't you think everybody would have one?

223. What exactly are life estates and how are they taxed when I die?

The recent popularity of life estates means that CPAs are frequently being asked to advise on their gift, estate, and income tax consequences. Here is an overview of the tax implications of life estates:

A life estate is a legal arrangement which allows one person to use, occupy, or enjoy property that belongs to someone else. In more practical terms it exists when an elderly parent—in legal terms, the "grantor"—wishes to give his or her home to an adult child while the parent retains the right to live in the house for the rest of his or her life. An attorney arranges to transfer the deed from the parent to the child, under the condition that the parent has the right to live there for life. People use life estates to remove property from their name and preserve it for heirs. Estate and income tax planning are also considerations.

If you're considering a life estate, you should carefully consider the tax consequences. In the most common example of a home, the owner of the life estate can either live in the home for life or have control over who can live there. This element of control (the life estate) may create an unexpected estate tax since the full value of the property, in this case, the house, is included in the estate of the person possessing the right of lifetime tenancy.

Depending on the size of the estate, a life estate can have estate tax advantages or disadvantages.

Example:
An 80 year-old father owns a home worth $130,000. It is the only asset in his estate. The original cost in 1948, plus improvements, is $10,000.

Step one:
The father transfers ownership of the home to his son, by deed, but retains the right to live in the home for life—a life estate.

Step two:
When the father dies, the home is included in his estate at its value of $130,000 and the son becomes the legal owner, with all life estate restrictions removed. At death there is no federal estate tax because of the 1997 $600,000 federal exemption from estate tax.

Step three:
The son sells the home for $130,000. No income tax to the son! Why? He is entitled to use the estate tax value of $130,000 as his cost basis for figuring gain, and since the selling price was also $130,000, there is no profit to tax. In addition, a commission paid to a real estate broker by the son would increase the cost basis and trigger a deductible loss. This would be a capital loss, since the home is not the son's residence, but rather is inherited property.

Had the father in the above example had a much larger estate, the life estate could have caused an estate tax problem. When this is the case, the father should consider ways of reducing his estate, such as a lifetime gifting program using the annual exclusions from gift tax (see *Question#20*).

Other issues
A life estate can also be used to protect the home for beneficiaries in second marriage situations, where, for example, your spouse is allowed to live in the home for life, but upon his or her death, it is bequeathed to your beneficiaries, not your spouse's.

You can also receive many of the estate and income tax advantages offered by a life estate by using an irrevocable trust to hold title. However, the trust would cost more in legal fees to set up than the life estate.

The following drawbacks to a life estate should be considered:
- *Grantor (most commonly the parent) loses control of the assets*
- *To sell the property in the life estate requires the consent of both parties*
- *Transfers made to qualify for Medicaid are illegal as of January 1, 1997* But only your attorney can go to jail, so who cares?

224 For a married couple, isn't the 1997 federal estate tax exemption $1.2 million? If my and my spouse's total estate is under this amount, then isn't it true that we'll have no federal estate tax?

Tax trap!

No. Unfortunately, this is what many people think, and that's why a couple with $1.2 million in assets who leave everything to each other, either through their will or with joint property, end up paying a large estate tax—$235,000—that could have been avoided.

The 1997 $600,000 exemption is the amount of assets that each person can pass free of estate taxes to their heirs. But it really has no applicability for passing property from one spouse to another following a death, because the marriage exemption means that such property generally is not subject to estate tax. Thus the exemption only applies when assets pass to someone other than the surviving spouse.

If, for example, a husband dies, leaving all his assets to his wife, he would have no estate and no estate tax, no matter how large his fortune. The problem is, if he has no assets passing to anyone other than the surviving spouse, he will not be able to use his 1997 $600,000 estate tax exemption, and if he does not use it, he loses it. His wife will inherit his assets, but not his exemption. She will be limited to her own 1997 $600,000 exemption, and will pay federal estate tax on anything above that. The couple, therefore, will only receive one 1997 $600,000 exemption, not the full $1,200,000 of estate tax protection they could have had if they had planned ahead and taken advantage of both their 1997 $600,000 exemptions.

225. I know that I can avoid all estate taxes on my death if I use the full marital deduction and leave everything to my spouse. Is there any reason that I should not take advantage of this most generous tax provision?

Yes. The term "marital deduction" is probably the most overused and poorly applied term in the estate planning area. The term refers to the fact that the surviving spouse pays no estate tax on property inherited from the deceased spouse, as mentioned in the question directly above. Most people think that by using the full marital deduction they have somehow "beat" the government out of a tax. The sad truth is that this is exactly what the government wants you to think, because it enables them to get the big bucks out of you later, at the second death, when you're no longer around to complain.

Tax trap!

Also, at the second death, when your children, who are now your executors, are writing that big fat check to IRS for estate taxes, they are probably wondering how you screwed this up. If your estate at the second death is $1.2 million or less, your executor should not even be writing a check, but they usually do because of the improper use of the unlimited marital deduction.

It turns out that the unlimited marital deduction is not that "generous." Patience may be a more apt description of the government's mind-set here. By using the full marital deduction, you have not avoided any estate tax—you have only deferred it until your spouse's death. Uncle Sam has no problem waiting around for your spouse to die because most times it's more than worth the wait.

The marital deduction is unlimited. It can be used to its full extent but does not have to be. Understanding its flexibility and taking advantage of the possibilities is where effective estate planning begins.

FACTORS TO CONSIDER
Taxes
If the only objective were to save estate taxes after the first death, then full use of the marital deduction would be advisable. However, it is important to keep in mind that the estate tax is not saved, but only deferred until the death of the surviving spouse.

Don't lose your exemption

The 1997 $600,000 exemption should be utilized in planning the appropriate use of the marital deduction. Losing the exemption is the single biggest mistake that is made in estate planning, resulting in a $235,000 federal estate tax that is avoidable. The key is to maximize the use of both spouses' exemptions. This can be done by designating assets up to the full amount of the exemption to pass to children or other worthy persons after the first spouse's death, either outright or through a credit shelter trust (see *Question #226*).

State estate taxes

State estate taxes must also be considered in determining the extent to which the marital deduction will be used. This is especially true where credit shelter trusts (see *Question #226*) are being used to maximize the exemption in the estate of the first spouse to die. In the state of New York, for example, the estate tax in 1997 on the first $600,000 of taxable assets is $25,500, because New York's exemption is only $115,000.

Other issues

The following issues should be explored, since they may have an impact on the extent to which the marital deduction should be used:

- *Is the surviving spouse competent to manage assets?*

- *What will the survivor need to live on? Is income enough or will principal also be needed? What invasion powers, if any, are being considered with regard to the principal?*

- *Health of the surviving spouse* What is the survivor's life expectancy? If the survivor is ill or has a short life expectancy, the full marital deduction should not be used since the exemption will be wasted.

- *Remarriage of the surviving spouse—is this an issue?* Will protection of your assets for your own family be a concern?

- *Is there a possibility of inheritance? And how large will the surviving spouse's estate be?*

- *What are the needs of other beneficiaries (children and grandchildren)? Are there any special needs to provide for, e.g., medical or educational?*

- *Does the survivor wish to reduce, gift, or consume his or her estate?*

226 **I've heard that a credit shelter trust can preserve the 1997 $600,000 exemption while still allowing a surviving spouse to enjoy dividends from financial assets or the use of real estate. What is a credit shelter trust?**

The credit shelter trust can be a testamentary trust (taking effect at death), or a revocable or irrevocable "living" trust which is set up and actually funded with property while you're alive. Each spouse can take up to the full 1997 $600,000 federal estate tax exemption and place it in a trust, designating beneficiaries, for example, children. After the first spouse dies, the surviving spouse retains the benefits of income from the assets of the trust (for example, stock or bonds) or use (if the assets are, for example, a house).

The credit shelter trust therefore accomplishes three purposes:

- *It secures the 1997 $600,000 estate tax exemption*

- *It keeps assets in trust while the surviving spouse is alive, so that it does not go directly to beneficiaries (for example, children) during the survivor's life*

- *It provides the surviving spouse with income from, or the benefits of, the trust property*

The credit shelter trust is extremely flexible since it includes property up to the 1997 $600,000 exemption that will then pass from the decedent's estate, tax-free. The trust usually works best if funded with assets whose appreciation potential are the greatest, since appreciation is free of estate tax. In smaller estates (under $600,000 for 1997), where the income, as well as possibly the principal, is being counted on for continued support of basic living expenses, the trust should be funded with liquid assets having income potential, since the beneficiaries may not be able to hold property long enough to realize the anticipated appreciation.

The reason most couples do not want assets going to the beneficiaries—usually the children—at the first death is they want to control those assets for the rest of their life, even if they do not technically own them. They are able to make investment decisions on trust assets, take certain allowable distributions, and provide a source of income for themselves. If the money had gone directly to a child, as an inheritance, the surviving spouse might have to depend on the child to provide income from the inherited assets.

The credit shelter trust is also variously referred to as the unified credit trust, the family trust, the non-marital trust, the bypass trust, or the credit shelter bypass trust.

Appendix A
What's the difference between?...

Alimony vs. child support
Alimony is paid to a former spouse. It is deductible by the one paying it, and must be reported as income by the one receiving it. *Child support* is neither deductible nor reportable as income. So if you're paying it, you want it to be alimony—and if you're receiving it, you want it to be child support.

Basis vs. cost
Cost is what you paid for property, whether a stock, a bond, a mutual fund or a home.

Basis, on the other hand, is the amount used for figuring any gain or loss when property is sold. To calculate basis, certain adjustments are added to or subtracted from your cost. Here are some examples:
- *For a home, the amount you pay for improvements will be added to the original price you paid, to arrive at an increased basis*
- *For a stock, any reinvested dividends on which you paid tax in the year they were earned will be added to the price you paid to arrive at an increased basis*
- *For a machine used in a business, any depreciation taken will be subtracted from the original price paid to arrive at a decreased basis*

Increasing basis results in a decrease in capital gains and the tax you'll pay, while decreasing basis results in an increase in capital gains and the tax you'll pay.

Capital gains vs. ordinary income
Capital gains are what everybody wants and *ordinary income* is what most people get. Capital gains result from the sale of what's called a "capital asset," which is generally anything you own, for example, a stock, a bond, mutual fund shares, or your home. Income from your trade or business is "ordinary." Ordinary income gets taxed at higher rates for many taxpayers. For example, if you're in a 36% tax bracket, you would pay 36% on ordinary income, whereas a capital gain would be taxed at a maximum of 20% if the property was held more than 18 months before it was sold.

Cash method vs. accrual method

These are the two general methods for reporting your income. The *cash method* means you report as income all moneys received and deposited within your tax year—generally the calendar year for individuals—and that you deduct as expenses all items paid within your tax year.

The *accrual method* is used mainly by businesses, especially those with inventory, receivables, and payables. Under the accrual method, income is reported when it is earned, for example, when the bill is sent out, not when you're actually paid. Expenses are deductible when they are incurred rather than when they are paid. For businesses, the accrual method has the advantage of more closely matching income to expenses.

Virtually all individual taxpayers use the cash method.

Estate tax vs. income tax

The *income tax* is the one you can still complain about.

Adjusted Gross Income vs. taxable income

It's important to know the difference between these two because so many provisions in the tax law are based on *Adjusted Gross Income* (AGI), not the income on which you are actually taxed. AGI is your gross income before any exemptions, deductions, or tax credits.

Deductible IRA vs. nondeductible IRA

A contribution to a *deductible IRA* is deductible for the tax year for which it is made and is taxed when withdrawn. A contribution to a *nondeductible IRA* receives no current tax deduction but is also not taxable when withdrawn. The traditional IRA is an example of an IRA which is deductible (as long as you're not eligible for a pension at work), while the new Roth and Education IRAs are examples of nondeductible IRAs.

Exclusion vs. deduction

An *exclusion* is something that you do not even have to include in your gross income. It never appears on your tax return. Examples are the proceeds from life insurance, gifts, or workmen's compensation; also salary deferrals made on a pre-tax basis, such as for a 401(k) plan.

A deduction, on the other hand, is an amount by which gross income is reduced. Examples include taxes paid to state or municipal authorities, and interest paid on your home mortgage.

Exemption vs. standard deduction

While both an *exemption* and a *standard deduction* are tax deductions, they serve different purposes. An exemption is a specified deduction based on how many dependents—including you and your spouse—you claim on your tax return. For 1997, each exemption is worth a $2,650 deduction. A standard deduction is a set deduction based on your filing status. You have a choice of taking it, or of itemizing deductible items. Generally, you should itemize unless you do not have enough deductions, or if certain special situations pertain.

Final tax return vs. estate tax return

The *final tax return* refers to your last income tax return, Form 1040, for the year of death.

The *estate tax return*, Form 706, is used to calculate how much estate tax is owed by the estate.

Fiscal year vs. calendar year

These are the terms referred to by businesses for tax reporting purposes. A *fiscal year* is a year that ends on any day other than December 31, whereas a *calendar year* is a year that ends on December 31.

Gift vs. bequest and gift tax vs. estate tax

A *gift* is something that you give while you are alive, whereas a *bequest* is something that you give upon death, through a will or a trust.

Gift tax is assessed on taxable gifts made during the donor's lifetime. The person who gives the gift is the person who has to pay the gift tax if there is one. Estate tax is a tax levied on an estate after death and is paid out of the estate.

The unified tax system in place for gift and estate tax is supposed to mean that whether you give it away while you are alive or it gets taxed in your estate, the tax will be the same. But it doesn't always happen that way: due to tax technicalities, paying a gift tax will cost you less than paying an estate tax on the same amount of property.

Independent contractor vs. employee

Independent contractor is what you, as a taxpayer, want to be, whereas *employee* is what the IRS wants you to be. To qualify as an independent contractor, you must generally be in your own business, working with your own tools, on your own schedule, and not under the control of the person who pays you; if not, that person or company is your employer. Generally, if you work for only one company, you are an employee of that company.

Joint tenancy vs. tenants in common
Both *joint tenancy* and *tenants in common* are ways for two or more people to share ownership of property. With joint tenancy, when one joint owner dies, the entire property goes to the surviving joint owner, without regard to any wills or trusts.

With tenants in common, when one joint owner dies, that joint owner's share goes to their own heirs through their will.

Using tenants in common protects joint owners who are not spouses and want to leave their shares of property to their own beneficiaries.

Long-term vs. short-term
These are terms used to describe the lengths of periods a stock, bond, or other capital asset is held, in order to determine whether a gain or loss is taxed at *short-term* or *long-term* rates. Higher tax is generally paid on short as opposed to long-term gains. For example, for capital gains, long-term means greater than 18 months (for more on this issue, see *Question #28*).

Qualified plan vs. non-qualified plan
A *qualified plan* is a type of employee benefit plan that meets prescribed IRS requirements. These requirements are complex and require paperwork, records and filings. Qualified plans offer tax advantages generally unavailable to non-qualified plans, including the fact that employers receive tax deductions for contributions to the plan made for the employees, and that employees pay no taxes on these contributions (which grow tax-deferred) until they are distributed, usually in retirement. Examples of qualified plans are: 401(k)s, 403(b)s, Defined Benefit Plans, Defined Contribution Plans, Keoghs, and Profit Sharing Plans.

Non-qualified plans are not required to meet the specific IRS requirements, but they do not enjoy the same tax benefits as qualified plans. So why would you want a non-qualified plan? Employers use non-qualified plans to provide special benefits not otherwise allowable to certain employees or executives. Non-qualified plans are also not subject to the spousal consent or discrimination rules.

Probate estate vs. taxable estate

The *probate estate* is the part of the estate, taxable or not, that is owned in the decedent's own name and passes through a will. It may be estate taxable or non-taxable.

The *taxable estate* is the amount of the estate that is subject to tax, and may include both probate property and non-probate property.

A house that is bequeathed by a deceased person's will to another is probate property and is taxable unless it, together with other items in the estate, is valued at less than the federal estate exemption. An IRA with a designated beneficiary is an example of non-probate property, and is included in the taxable estate.

S corporation vs. C corporation

There are two types of business corporations. Every corporation is a *C corporation* when formed and remains so, until and unless, an *S corporation* election is filed with the IRS on Form 2553. The two corporation types are named "C" and "S" after the sections of the Internal Revenue Code which bear these letter codes.

C corporations pay corporation tax on profits, while S corporations' profits or losses are passed through to the personal tax returns of the S corporation shareholders. Losses by S corporations may be deductible on the personal returns of the S corporation shareholders. Most smaller businesses who incorporate elect to be S corporations.

Surviving spouse vs. qualifying widow(er)

A *qualifying widow(er)* may use joint tax return rates for up to two years after the death of a spouse. To be entitled to this benefit you must have a dependent. A *surviving spouse* is the same thing but without the tax benefit.

Tax audit vs. tax examination

There is no difference. They both stink.

Tax avoidance vs. tax evasion

Tax avoidance is legal; *tax evasion* isn't. For example, this book will help you to avoid some of the taxes you are currently paying. That's legal tax avoidance. Many times the difference between the two is small enough that a judge must decide whether a particular strategy amounts to avoidance or evasion.

Tax bill vs. tax law

A *tax bill* is what everyone says the law will be (but don't bet on it). A *tax law* is what the law actually is.

Tax credit vs. tax deduction

A *tax credit* is much more valuable because it is a direct, dollar for dollar, reduction of your tax. A *tax deduction* is a reduction of your taxable income, the amount subject to tax.

Tax-free vs. tax-deferred

Tax-free means you will never pay income tax on it. *Tax-deferred* means you won't pay income tax now, but you must pay later. For example, retirement accounts are tax-deferred. You do not pay income tax on the income earned in these accounts until withdrawn, but once the moneys are withdrawn, they are subject to tax because the deferral is over.

Tax tables vs. tax rate schedules

Both the *tax tables* and the *tax rate schedules* are used to figure the tax you must pay. For people with taxable income of less than $100,000, you can generally use the tax tables, which means you just have to look up under the right filing status and the right income amount to determine your tax. If your income is $100,000 or higher, you must use the tax rate schedules, which require you to do some computations to arrive at your tax.

Transfer vs. rollover

A direct *transfer* occurs when you move funds from one IRA account to another. A *rollover*, on the other hand, occurs when you take money from a qualified plan, for example, your company pension plan or a 401(k), and move it to an IRA, an IRA rollover account, or another company's qualified plan.

You can execute as many transfers as you like, as long as the funds go from trustee to trustee (the trustee is the bank, brokerage, or mutual fund you've invested the moneys with) and are not paid to you directly. There is no tax on transfers because the money never comes out of the account.

Rollovers can be executed only once a year; the annual period starts on the day of the first rollover.

Appendix B How the new tax law treats IRA withdrawals

Withdrawals made before age 59½

For	TRADITIONAL IRA 10% penalty?	TRADITIONAL IRA Taxable?	FUNDS IN A ROTH IRA FOR LESS THAN fIVE YEARS 10% penalty?	FUNDS IN A ROTH IRA FOR LESS THAN fIVE YEARS Taxable?	FUNDS IN A ROTH IRA FOR fIVE OR MORE YEARS 10% penalty?	FUNDS IN A ROTH IRA FOR fIVE OR MORE YEARS Taxable?
Higher education	No	Yes	No	On earnings, not original contributions	No	On earnings, not original contributions
First time homebuyer ($10,000 lifetime max)	No	Yes	No	On earnings, not original contributions	No	No
Disability or death	No	Yes	No	On earnings, not original contributions	No	No
For any other reason	Yes, but there are some exceptions*	Yes	On earnings, not original contributions	On earnings, not original contributions	On earnings, not original contributions	On earnings, not original contributions

Withdrawals made at or after age 59½

For	TRADITIONAL IRA 10% penalty?	TRADITIONAL IRA Taxable?	FUNDS IN A ROTH IRA FOR LESS THAN fIVE YEARS 10% penalty?	FUNDS IN A ROTH IRA FOR LESS THAN fIVE YEARS Taxable?	FUNDS IN A ROTH IRA FOR fIVE OR MORE YEARS 10% penalty?	FUNDS IN A ROTH IRA FOR fIVE OR MORE YEARS Taxable?
For any reason	No	Yes	No	On earnings, not original contributions	No	No

*Exceptions include:
- Withdrawals for medical expenses
- If you become unemployed
- If you choose to annuitize withdrawals

See *Question #184* for further discussion.

Acknowledgments

For a long time I have wanted to write a book that could provide people with direct answers to the tax questions I have heard over the years from clients and friends. And now I have finally done it. But it would have never been possible without the encouragement and support of my wonderful publishers, Bill and Frank Berk, the heart and soul of Plymouth Press, Ltd. Bill and Frank are about as hands-on as you can get. They loved the idea and saw it through. Thanks guys!

I must acknowledge the various professionals who helped with the many technical points. It's a real task to take tax law this complicated, digest it, and present in an easy-to-use and understand format.

My thanks to my friend, Attorney Joseph Imbasciani, whose expertise in the estate planning area was invaluable. Joe Imbasciani is the most careful and meticulous attorney I have known. His estate planning clients are lucky. Working and giving seminars with Joe and Christine (Joe's wife and office manager) is both fun and rewarding.

Probably the single toughest area of tax law is the IRA and pension area. Special thanks to my friend, attorney, and CPA, Seymour Goldberg, for his guidance. "Sy" is a national guru on IRA's. He is also the author of several IRA books, including the popular and authoritative J.K. Lasser's *How to Pay Less Tax on Your Retirement Savings*.

Most accountants have learned something about taxes from the "Tax Master" himself, Sidney Kess, CPA, Esq. I am no exception. However, I have had the added privilege and honor to share the lectern with Sidney on several national and local tax conferences, including the AICPA's annual *"Tax Strategies for the High Income Individual"* conference held in Las Vegas, one of my favorites. I thank Sidney for including me in these programs, and for the personal and professional mentoring and advice he has generously given me.

Thanks, also, to my fellow CPAs at the New York State Society of Certified Public Accountants (NYSSCPA's). As a past chairman and member of the NYSSCPA's Estate Planning Committee, I have learned the value of being active with this group of highly skilled CPAs. Becoming involved with this organization was the single most productive decision of my professional life. These people are not just colleague CPA's, but friends, educators, and problem solvers. They are:

Nadine Gordon Lee, CPA, Senior Vice President, U.S. Trust Company

Laurence I. Foster, CPA/PFS, Partner, KPMG Peat Marwick LLP

Joseph V. Falanga, CPA, Partner, Goldstein Golub Kessler & Co., P.C.

Raymond G. Russolillo, CPA/PFS, CFP, Director, Personal Financial Services, Price Waterhouse LLP

Alan Kahn, CPA, The AJK Financial Group

Melvin I. Feit, CPA

Bertram Gezelter, Esq., CPA

Mark I. Rozell, Esq., CPA

Susan R. Schoenfeld, Esq., CPA

Larry Elkin, CPA, author of **Financial Self Defense for Unmarried Couples** (Doubleday)

Stanley Ross, Esq., CPA

Joseph Saslaw, CPA

Max Wasser, CPA

Richard H. Sonet, Esq., CPA

Jerry Landau, Esq., CPA

Ginger Broderick, CPA

James B. McEvoy, CPA

Janice M. Johnson, JD, CPA, D.S. Wolf Associates, Inc.

James L. Craig, Jr., CPA, Managing Editor, *The CPA Journal*

Menachem "Mike" Rosenberg, CPA, Margolin, Winer & Evens LLP

Barry C. Picker, CPA, CFP

Franklin H. Federmann, CPA

Lawrence M. Lipoff, CPA, CEBS

Phillip P. Drudy, CPA, Esq., Grant Thornton LLP

The National Conference of CPA Practitioners (NCCPAP) is a dedicated group of nationwide small firm CPAs who help each other and promote the value of CPAs to businesses and individuals. I have had the honor and opportunity to serve on the Board of Directors of the Nassau/Suffolk Chapter where I met and became friends with many fellow CPAs. Thanks to you all:

Arlene Harmon, Education Director
Jack Weisbrod, CPA, President 1997-1998
Arthur Libman, CPA, past President
Rhona Liptzin, CPA, past President
Alan Brooks, CPA, past President
Carol Markman, CPA, past President
John Giunta, CPA
Karen Giunta, CPA
Stan Tepper, CPA
Stuart G. Lang, CPA
Michael Winnick, CPA

I cannot forget my favorite financial writer, Lynn Brenner. When it comes to writing, Lynn is my mentor. She has such a wonderful talent of making the most complicated topics easy for everyone to understand. I would be happy to have one tenth of her writing skills. She writes for *Newsday* and for numerous other financial publications which are lucky enough to feature her work. She is also the author of **Smart Questions to Ask Your Financial Advisers** (Bloomberg Press, 1997). She had the guts to be my very first radio show guest. Thanks Lynn!

I was fortunate to have the assistance of Alice Bredin, an internationally recognized authority on the small office/home office (SOHO) market. She writes the widely syndicated column, *"Working At Home."* Alice Bredin is the ultimate entrepreneur, a consultant who actually practices what she preaches. I admire her spirit and enthusiasm. She is also the author of *The Virtual Office Survival Handbook* and *Home Office Solutions* (John Wiley & Sons, Inc.).

Thanks to my friends at *News 12 Long Island* who put me in front of the TV cameras each week. Nothing helps build confidence better than live TV! Thanks to Pat Dolan, the news director, and producer Robert Licata for their guidance, and for giving me the opportunity to provide weekly financial advice to thousands of Long Islanders. Special thanks to my *On the Money* producer, Naomi Lipstein, and to news anchors, Doug Geed and Carol Silva (in my humble opinion, the world's nicest person), and to the rest of the morning gang who make it look so easy.

Acknowledgments

Someone had to help make *Your Tax Questions Answered* both readable and accurate, and for that I thank Paula Licata and Raymond G. Russolillo, CPA/PFS. Paula Licata is not only a great typist and writer, but her editing skills proved invaluable.

Ray Russolillo of Price Waterhouse is one of the nation's top tax experts. He made sure *Your Tax Questions Answered* not only reads well but that it is technically correct, a job I could not have done alone. Thanks, Ray, for your input and your friendship…and for guest hosting *The Money Show* for me. I like listening to you more than listening to myself.

I also want especially to thank the following people for their stellar comments on the manuscript of this book: Melvin I. Feit, Barry C. Picker, and Laurence I. Foster.

Without the hard work of a an energetic publicist you might not be reading this. Shari L. Goldstein is a public relations machine that keeps on going and going…just like that battery bunny. Shari heads up her own public relations firm in Huntington, NY. Thank you, Shari, for the terrific job you do!

Your Tax Questions Answered would not have been possible without the support of Margot Reilly and Laurin Levine. Margot and Laurin make sure our accounting firm and our clients are well taken care of, day in and day out…even on weekends. I could not ask for two more dedicated, loyal, and competent people to work with. Thanks also to our tax department, Edward Schwartzman and Michael Lichter, who provided useful ideas and practical advice for the book. They also help make tax season a little easier on all of us.

About 20 years ago a couple of great CPAs gave me my first real job as an accountant. I want to thank Sidney Markowitz and Bernard Siegel for that opportunity. My years at Markowitz & Siegel were the best education money couldn't buy. They taught me well, and I have the greatest respect for them both.

Finally, as any good son should do, I thank my parents, Bob and Beverly Slott, for instilling confidence, and for their unwavering support, no matter what harebrained idea I got myself involved with. They were always there. My father, a CPA himself, gave me the idea to go into accounting with his observation, "It's not a bad way to make a living." He was right! Thanks Dad.

Index

A
accountant
  small businesses and 90
accrual method
  defined 198
adopting children
  tax credits for 67
amended returns 20, 21
ancillary probate 187
Annual Report of Earnings
  Social Security benefits and 175
annuities
  variable 16
audits 139
  accountant and 144
  appeals of 141
  divorce and 121
  IRS criteria for initiating 137
  preparation for 140, 142
  worst mistake in 144
auto/truck expenses
  for business 86, 89

B
basis 23, 42, 44, 45, 97, 133, 191, 197
  defined 197
bequest
  defined 199
business
  auto/truck expenses 86, 89
  deductions 86, 88
  equipment 87
  estate tax and 186
  expenses, direct vs. indirect 72
  failure and capital losses 89
  failure and deductions 89
  incorporation of 81, 82
  insurance 87
  liability 82
  meals/entertainment 86
  office supplies 87
  payroll 87
  property, sale of 96
  start-up costs and 88
  telephone 86
  travel expenses 86
bypass trust. *See* credit shelter trust

C
C corporation(s)
  defined 201
  profits and taxation 85
capital gains 16, 28
  defined 197
  home, exclusion from 127
  home sales and
    121, 125, 126, 127, 128, 129, 133
  municipal bonds and 38
  stock sales and 39
carryovers
  business expenses and 73
  losses and 48
cash method
  defined 198
charitable contributions
  donated blood and 60
  clothes and 59
  deduction of expenses related to charity work and 60
  deductions for work done and 60
  documenting for tax returns 61
  goods received for 61
  household items and 59
  maximum annual 62
  receipts for 22
  services received for 61
charity
  qualified
    defined 60
child care providers 24
child support 123
  unmarried couples and 109
Child Tax Credit 66
children
  employment of 92
collectibles
  IRA rules and 158

college expenses 57
corporations 81, 82, 83
  C 82
  S 83
cost
  defined 197
credit shelter trusts 194, 195, 196

D

death
  benefit 160
  IRA withdrawals and 204
deduction(s)
  accelerating 63
  home office and audits 79
  blood donated and 60
  business 86, 88
  business auto/truck expenses 86, 89
  business equipment and 87, 93, 95, 96
  business failure and 89
  checking last year's return for 25
  children and 66
  clothes contributions and 59
  defined 198, 202
  depreciation and 27
  education costs and 52
  expenses related to charity work 60
  home office and tutoring 76
  home mortgage 49
  home office 72, 73, 76
  home office and sale of home 78
  home office, qualifying for 77
  household item contributions and 59
  job hunting expenses and 51, 52
  late claims and 19
  losses and 51
  miscellaneous and 2% limit 65, 101
  missed 21
  organizing 22
  points on mortgages 50
  Schedule A and 64
  tax shelters and 69
  teaching and home office deduction 75
  trusts and 64
  2% limit 65

  work for charities and 60
Delayed Retirement Credits
  Social Security benefits and 175
dependents 138
depreciation
  defined 88
  home 132
  recapture 96, 131, 133
    home office and 76
disability
  insurance
    income from 37
  IRA withdrawals and 148, 149, 151, 204
distribution methods
  IRAs 162, 164, 165
distribution rules
  IRAs 162
dividends
  reinvested, deduction of 47
divorce 105
  audit and 121
  filing options and 106
  homes and 121
  legal fees and 117
  pension distribution and 119
  tax liability and 122
  timing of for tax purposes 117

E

education 53, 56
  IRA 54
  paying for with IRA 148, 149, 151, 204
  tax credits 53, 54, 55, 57
education IRAs 103
employee(s)
  defined 199
  hiring for small business 90
  taxes related to 90
entertainment
  business 86
equipment
  business 87, 95
  business deductions 95, 96
estate tax 44, 115, 185
  deduction 169

defined 198, 199
  emigrating abroad and 183
  exemption 181
  federal exemption from
    192, 193, 194, 195
  marital deduction and 193, 194, 195
  second home and 134
estate tax return
  defined 199
estimated tax payments 26, 28, 41
  divorce and 119
exclusion
  defined 198
executor's fees
  taxation of 43
exemption(s)
  child and divorce 120
  defined 199
  marriage penalty and 100
  personal 66, 69
extension for filing returns 21

F
family farm
  estate tax and 186
family trust. *See* credit shelter trust
farm
  estate tax and 186
Federal Unemployment Tax (FUTA) 92
FICA
  business employees and 86, 91
filing status
  married couples and 104, 106
final tax return
  defined 199
first-year expensing
  business deductions and 93, 95, 96
fiscal year
  defined 199
form
  706 199
  940 92
  940-EZ 92
  941 91
  942 30

1040 29, 38, 85, 119, 199
1040X 19
1041 189
1099 23, 138
1099-INT 119
1099-LTC 63
1120-X 85
1127 21
2119 14
2553 83, 201
4562 93
8109 91
8283 59, 139
8332 120
8379 24, 123
8506 153
8822 25, 118
8829 72, 73, 77
8839 69
9465 21
I-9 30, 91
SS-5 24
SSA-777-SM 175
W-2 15, 24, 26, 30, 93, 94, 95, 138
W-3 30
401(k) plan(s) 98
  borrowing from 154

G
gift tax
  defined 199
gift(s) 35, 36, 58
  as a tax strategy 112, 114
  deduction of 58
  defined 199
gold
  IRAs and 158
grantor trust 189

H
health care proxy 180
health insurance
  deductions 87
hearing impaired
  IRS resource for 17

hobby losses
  IRS audit and 139
home equity loans 16, 49, 57
home mortgage 15
  deductions 49, 50
  gifting with 58
  refinancing 49
  unmarried couples and 114
home office 130, 131
  sale of home and 131
home office deduction 72, 73, 76, 77
  audits and 79
  capital gain from home sale and 78
  renting and 76
home(s)
  business use of 129, 130
  divorce and 121
  IRA distribution for purchase of
    148, 149, 151, 204
  sale of
    125, 126, 127, 129, 130, 131, 133
  second 133, 134, 136
  unmarried couples and 108, 109,
    112, 113, 114
HOPE Scholarship Tax Credit 53, 55, 57
  divorce and 120
household employees
  taxes and 29–31

I

income
  deferring 63
Income in Respect of a Decedent (IRD) 170
income tax
  business 84
  defined 198
  withholding employees' 91
incorporation
  business 81, 82
independent contractor(s) 92
  defined 199
injured spouse
  relief 123
innocent spouse 122

installment sales 27
insurance
  business 87
  health 87
  life. *See* life insurance
  long term care 62
interest income
  divorce and 119
IRA(s)
  annuitizing before age 59½ 156
  beneficiary selection 165
  borrowing from 157, 158
  collectibles and 158
  contributing late to 152
  contributing to in golden years 152
  contribution due date 145
  deductibility and Social Security 177
  deductibility limits 103
  deductible vs. nondeductible 198
  distributions from 148-149,
    160, 162, 164-168, 204
  education 56
  gold and 158
  home-buying and withdrawals from
    151, 152
  hybrid distribution method 162, 165
  inherited, tax on 169, 175
  life insurance and 158
  married couples and 100
  medical expenses and 157
  Minimum Distribution Incidental Benefit
    Rule and 164
  once calculated distribution method 162
  penalties 166, 167, 169
  prohibited transactions and 157, 159
  recalculation distribution method 162
  rollover(s) 23, 155, 168
  Roth 103
    converting to 146, 148
    general explanation of 146
    withdrawals from 204
  silver and 158
  spouse's 153
  term certain distribution method 162, 164

withdrawals *See* IRA(s): distributions from
irrevocable living trust. *See* living trust
irrevocable trust 184
IRS
    help in tax preparation 17
    internet site 17

J
job hunting expenses
    deduction of 51, 52
joint tenancy
    defined 200

L
legal fees
    divorce and 117
life estates 190, 192
    defined 190
life insurance
    beneficiaries of 37
    estate planning and 180
    estates and 183, 184
    IRAs and 158
    transferring beneficiaries of 184
    unmarried couples and 110, 115
Lifetime Learning Credit 54, 55, 57
    divorce and 120
limited liability corporation 82
    profits and taxation 84, 85
limited partnerships 16
living together agreement 108
living trust(s) 180, 181, 184, 187-190
    advantages of 187
    defined 187
    gifting from 189
living will
    unmarried couples and 110
long term care insurance 62
long-term
    defined 200
loss carryovers 48
losses
    deducting 51
    theft/casualty 101

M
MACRS (Modified Accelerated Cost Recovery) 133
marital deduction
    federal estate tax and 193, 194, 195
marriage
    annullment of 118
    filing options and 104, 106
    head of household, and 105
    Social Security benefits and 176
marriage bonus 102
marriage penalty 99
    spouses' businesses and 95
married
    filing jointly 104
    filing separately 105
meals
    business 86
medical dependent
    unmarried couples and 111
medical expenses 120, 121
    IRAs and 157
    married couples and 101
    Social Security benefits and 177
    unmarried couples and 110
medical insurance
    unmarried couples and 109
Medical Savings Accounts (MSAs) 170
Medicare tax 86
    employees and 91
Minimum Distribution Incidental Benefit Rule
    IRAs and 164
mixed use property 135
mortgage *See* home mortgage
municipal bonds 28
    capital gains from 38
mutual funds
    capital gains from 41–43

N
name change 118
    notifying IRS of 25
Nanny Tax 29

net operating losses 26, 85
no-nuptial agreements 108
non-marital trust. *See* credit shelter trust
non-probatable property 182
non-qualified plan
   defined 200

O

office supplies
   business and 87
once calculated
   IRA distribution option 162
ordinary income
   defined 197

P

passive activity losses 26
payroll
   business 87
pension(s). *See also* IRA(s), 401(k)
   layoffs and 155
   rollovers 23
   unmarried couples and 110
power of attorney
   durable 180
   unmarried couples and 110
probate 187, 189
   ancillary 187
   defined 181
probate estate
   defined 201
prohibited transactions
   IRA 157
property tax 38

Q

qualified plan
   defined 200
qualifying widow(er)
   defined 201

R

real estate sales
   capital gains from 40

real estate tax 38
recalculation
   IRA distribution option 162, 165
record date
   for stock sales 42
reinvested dividends
   deduction of 47
retirement. *See* IRA(s), pension(s), 401(k)
retirement death benefit 160
revocable living trust. *See* living trust
rollover (IRA)
   defined 202
Roth IRA. *See* IRA(s): Roth

S

S corporation(s) 83
   defined 201
   election 83, 84
   profits and taxation 84
SARSEP retirement plans 172
savings bonds 37
Schedule
   A 64, 65, 72, 73
   B 119
   C 20, 53, 85, 137
   H 29, 30
self-employment tax 84, 85, 86
short-term
   defined 200
silver
   IRAs and 158
SIMPLE retirement plans 172
Social Security benefits 28
   Annual Report of Earnings and 175
   Delayed Retirement Credits and 175
   medical expenses and 177
   tax-exempt income and 177
   taxation of 174, 177
   timing the start of 174
   working and 173, 175
Social Security number(s) 118
   dependents and 24
sole proprietorships 82
   profits and taxation 84, 85

standard deduction 69, 102
  defined 199
state income tax
  deduction of on federal returns 48
  refund 35
stock sales
  capital gains from 39, 41
  gifted stock and 45
  inherited stock and 44
  sell slips and 23
student loan interest
  deduction of 54, 56, 57, 103
suits (legal)
  damage awards from 38
surviving spouse
  defined 201

T

tax
  audit
    defined 201
  avoidance
    defined 202
  credit(s)
    child 104
    defined 202
  deferred
    defined 202
  evasion
    defined 202
  examination
    defined 201
  exempt income
    Social Security benefits and 176, 177
  free
    defined 202
  records, how long to keep 13
  returns
    how long to keep 13
    when to stop filing 32
  shelter(s) 69
taxable estate
  defined 201

teaching
  home office deduction and 75
telephone
  business 86
tenants in common
  defined 200
term certain
  IRA distribution option 162, 164
testamentary trust 187
transfer (IRA)
  defined 202
travel
  business 86
trusts
  deductibility of costs associated with 64

U

U.S. Savings Bonds 37
unemployment insurance 28
unmarried couples
  child support and 109
  cohabitation agreement and 108
  homes and 108, 109, 112, 113, 114
  life insurance and 110, 115
  living together agreements and 108
  living will and 110
  medical expenses and 109, 110-112
  no-nuptial agreements and 108
  pensions and 110
  power of attorney and 110
  real estate tax and 114
  wills and 110

W

wills 181, 183, 188
  deductibility of costs associated with 64
  unmarried couples and 108, 110
withholding taxes 91

About the Author

A nationally recognized tax expert, Edward A. Slott, CPA is a contributor to *The CPA Journal, The Practical Accountant, Tax Hotline, The Tax Adviser,* and other tax newsletters and periodicals. He is frequently quoted by *The New York Times, Washington Post, The Los Angeles Times, USA Today, Newsday, Newsweek, Fortune, Forbes, Money,* and other important financial publications. He has appeared on CNBC, ABC, NBC, and PBS.

Ed lectures widely on taxes, personal financial planning, IRAs and retirement planning, and estate planning to audiences of CPAs, attorneys, financial consultants, business groups, charitable organizations, and the general public. He co-hosts the *"Protect Your Wealth"* estate planning seminars, held monthly on Long Island. He is also coauthor of the *"Practice Building Success Strategies for Attorneys,"* a national seminar series and manual.

Ed hosts *The Money Show with Ed Slott, CPA,* a weekly radio program, and is the financial correspondent for News 12 Long Island, hosting their weekly *On the Money* feature.

Ed is a principal in the accounting firm of E. Slott & Company, 100 Merrick Road, Rockville Centre, NY 11570. He lives in Oceanside, New York…where he grew up and was married.

Ed Slott's IRA Advisor
Newsletter

Ed Slott's IRA Advisor is a unique newsletter that addresses the complex issues of IRAs, retirement planning, and estate planning in the easy-to-understand style that has earned Ed Slott a national audience of taxpayers and tax professionals. You'll enjoy having Ed explain the new Roth IRAs, 401 (k)s, 403 (b)s, Keoghs, and traditional IRAs with refreshing wit and clarity. Protect your life savings with **Ed Slott's IRA Advisor**. Annual subscription (12 issues) is $79.95. Call (516) 536-8282 to order or for a sample issue.

Protect Your Wealth™
Estate planning seminars

Ed Slott and Attorney Joseph Imbasciani present monthly *Protect Your Wealth™* estate planning seminars. For more information, call (516) 536-8282.

Unanswered Questions?

Have a tax question that wasn't answered by this book? Or any suggestions? Please send them to: Plymouth Press, 42500 Five Mile Road, Plymouth, MI 48170, or you can E-mail Ed at SlottCPA@AOL.com.. If we use your question or idea in the next edition of Your Tax Questions Answered, we'll credit you in writing and send you a free copy.

Your Tax Questions Answered
• Order form •

Please send me:

_____ copies of Your Tax Questions Answered   Each $11.95 _____

Michigan residents add 6% sales tax _____

Vermont residents add 5% sales tax _____

Ship to: Total _____

_____
Name

_____
Address

_____
City/State/Zip

Credit card orders: MasterCard/Visa (800) 350-1007

Checks payable to: Plymouth Press. **Enclose order form with payment.**

Send to: Plymouth Press
          101 Panton Road
          Vergennes, VT 05491